Joseph Schmertz, Son —

December 5/65

"Go ye therefore, and teach all nations, baptizing them in the name of the Father, and of the Son, and of the Holy Ghost:

Teaching them to observe all things whatsoever I have commanded you: and, lo, I am with you alway, even unto the end of the world."

MATTHEW 28: 19-20

Six Missions of Texas

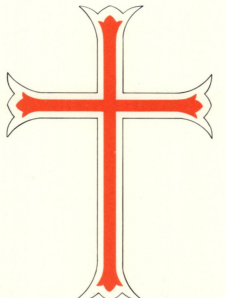

Introduction by

GOVERNOR JOHN CONNALLY

Preface by

HONORABLE PRICE DANIEL

Historical Coordinator

DORMAN H. WINFREY

JAMES DAY

JOE B. FRANTZ

BEN PROCTER

JOSEPH W. SCHMITZ

LON TINKLE

DORMAN H. WINFREY

TEXIAN PRESS　　•　　1965　　•　　WACO, TEXAS

Library of Congress Catalog Card Number
65-27835

First Edition

Published
by

P. O. Box 1684
Waco, Texas

Bound by
Library Binding Co.
Waco, Texas

The mission padres who as messengers of Christ were among the first white men to compete with Nature for the untamed land that came to be Texas. As they sought to Christianize the Indians of the Southwest, they opened the country for white man's civilization. This volume is a tribute to their toil.

Introduction

Texas is the owner of the beautiful paintings of six selected missions of our State because the donors, John B. and Veree McFadin Godfrey, Austin, visited an "interesting old mission" while touring California in April, 1956.

Mr. and Mrs. Godfrey, then residents of Portland, Oregon, saw in the San Francisco Solano Desonoma mission a part of our heritage that should renew our strength in our ancestors. They remembered that the missions of Texas were even more precious in man's memory. Mrs. Godfrey visioned then that an outstanding artist should preserve the missions on canvas for the permanent preservation of their individuality.

Nothing was done toward the project until the Godfreys retired and returned to their native Texas in 1958. Early in 1962 Mrs. Godfrey, whose grandfather, David H. McFadin, fought in the Texas Revolution, along with General Sam Houston, President Mirabeau B. Lamar and other Texas patriots, had a conversation with the late James Bradford Card, owner of Austin's Country Store and Art Gallery. Mr. Card pursued the suggestion that such a work of art should be commissioned and presented to our State. Many of the leading artists of the Southwest were contacted and asked to present oil paintings of their choice of the missions. Before the artist was selected, Mr. Card died and ownership of the Country Store changed to Mr. and Mrs. John H. Jenkins and Associates. One of the associates and veteran employee of the firm, Mr. Carl Barho, had been watching the work of the artist, Granville Bruce, who had been commissioned by the Parks and Wildlife Commission to paint the natural scenery background for the wildlife exhibit area of the John H. Reagan Building. Mr. and Mrs. Godfrey became acquainted with Mr. Bruce, and they suggested that he should paint the missions.

The work of Mr. Bruce was exactly what Mr. and Mrs. Godfrey had been searching for and he was commissioned to paint six missions selected by the Godfreys: La Bahía of Goliad, and Concepción, San José, San Francisco de Espada, San Juan de Capistrano and the Alamo, all of San Antonio. Thus, the long-dreamed of goal of the Godfreys has culminated into a rare and valuable gift to our State and an important acquisition to the Texas State Library.

As one can trace the history of the Lone Star State through its historic missions, so may one trace the great love the Godfreys have for their State through their ancestors.

Mrs. Veree McFadin Godfrey, a native of Williamson County, was born at Circleville, some six miles north of Taylor. She is the daughter of Judge and Mrs. John Newen (Mollie Teague Sherman) McFadin who served as chief justice of Williamson County and district attorney of the Western District of Texas. Her paternal grandfather, David Hutcheson McFadin, fought in the Texas Revolution. The McFadin ancestors are of Scotch-Irish lineage, who settled in Ulster in 1607 and emigrated to America after 1718. Her maternal grandfather was William P. Sherman, who was in the merchandising business and also a veteran of the Texas Revolution. The Shermans came to Texas from Ohio.

Mrs. Godfrey joined the Daughters of the Republic of Texas in 1904. Her DRT certificate was signed by a charter member of the organization, Mrs. Anson Jones, wife of the last president of the Republic of Texas. She is the oldest "paid-up" member in the organization today.

Mr. and Mrs. Godfrey were married in 1912 in Austin at the Driskill Hotel in the Hogg Memorial Room. He was then a salesman for the Nelson-Davis Grocery Company.

Mr. Godfrey is a native of Grayson County, having been born near Whitesboro. His parents were pioneers of the area, having emigrated to Texas from Missouri and Mississippi prior to the Civil War. He was graduated from the Carlisle Military Academy.

Mr. and Mrs. Godfrey moved to Florida in 1924 and in 1928 a business opportunity in Portland, Oregon, caused them to move across the nation. They made their home in Portland for 30 years where Mr. Godfrey was in the insurance business.

Mr. Granville Bruce, the artist, resides in Irving and received his early training at the Layton School of Art, Chicago and the Chicago Art Institute. In San Antonio Mr. Bruce met Hugo D. Pohl, a recognized art instructor and craftsman, and after intensive study under Mr. Pohl, the student and teacher decided to establish an art studio in the heart of Brackenridge Park Zoo. During 1928 Mr. Bruce organized a class in landscape painting, and although Brackenridge Park offered almost endless scenes for study, the favorite subjects of students and instructor were the missions.

The field of commercial illustrating beckoned to Mr. Bruce, and in 1931 he began a long career of service to such publications as *Farm and Ranch, Holland's Magazine, The Progressive Farmer* and many others.

Later he expanded into architectural delineation. Since 1933 Mr. Bruce has been the staff artist for the Dallas Museum of Natural History.

John Connally
Governor of Texas

Preface

Among the responsibilities charged by law to the Texas Library and Historical Commission are directives to "collect materials relating to the history of Texas . . . encourage historical work and research" and to "diffuse knowledge in regard to the history of Texas."

The generous donations of the paintings of the Six Missions of Texas to the Texas State Library by Mr. and Mrs. John B. Godfrey and this publication of the history of the missions greatly assist the Texas Library and Historical Commission in fulfilling its responsibility to the people of Texas. The missions displayed in the Reference Division of the Texas State Library can be seen by school children, visitors, tourists, and other interested persons who wish to view an important aspect of the history of this State. The reproductions of the missions along with the historical texts can be made available in printed form to schools, libraries, and to individuals.

The Texian Press of Waco, under the direction of Robert E. Davis, has the thanks and appreciation of the Texas Library and Historical Commission for undertaking this publication. The Texian Press has done much to help the Commission disseminate Texas history. Last year another such undertaking produced the highly acclaimed *Heroes of Texas*, historical biographies along with reproductions of the Summerfield G. Roberts' "Texas Hero Portraits."

Our State is fortunate to have citizens like Mr. and Mrs. Godfrey and the publishers and authors of this book, who have the love and appreciation of the Texas heritage and the desire to make a part of their State's history available in this manner.

Price Daniel
Texas Library and Historical Commission

Acknowledgment

Texian Press is indebted to the authors of this book, who took time from busy schedules to prepare the history of each mission. To Mr. and Mrs. John B. Godfrey who commissioned the paintings and presented them to the State Library. Our special thanks to Dorman H. Winfrey, State Librarian, who not only wrote the history of San Francisco de Espada but also acted as historical co-ordinator for the entire book. It was Dr. Winfrey who first brought the beautiful paintings to our attention, and to him goes the credit for the basic idea of publishing this volume. The Texas Library and Historical Commission for making the original paintings available for reproduction. Colonel Harold B. Simpson for his valuable help as historical consultant. Bob Abernathy for his excellent drawing of the Spanish cross used on the title page and front cover. Marion Travis of Waco and Dorothy Blodgett of Austin for their valuable editorial advice. Mr. Irvin Lynn for his beautiful design of the dust jacket, and Paul Loftin, who has encouraged every project and publication of Texian Press. There are many others, too numerous to mention, whose skill and craftsmanship transformed the original idea to the finished book.

Texian Press

Table of Contents

The Alamo

The Alamo

The Alamo

by

Lon Tinkle

Of all the approximately forty missions established in Texas, the Alamo is the only one not called after the saint in whose honor it was founded. It is the only Texas mission whose chief gift to history lay outside its religious purpose, the only one whose major role transcended its association with the trinity of institutions by which Spain civilized and organized the "Indies": Mission, Pueblo, Presidio.

Uniquely, it was also each of these institutions. It is a mission that became a fort—remembered more for its symbolic value in battle than for its share in the salvation of souls. Its symbolic value allows it the designation, "pueblo." If not literally a township, the Alamo was a community of political spirit and aspiration; and, later, a community of freedom-loving souls. Texans think of it first, not as fort, nor as mission, but as a concrete symbol of Liberty.

William Barret Travis thought of the Alamo in this way when Liberty was most desperately menaced. In his famous letter "To The Texans And All Americans In The World," announcing that, "I will never surrender or retreat," he called for help "in the name of Liberty." Although less religious in its associations than the other missions, the Alamo *is* a spiritual emblem, quite properly known as "The Cradle of Texas Liberty."

With a kind of magic, the Alamo drew great men and powerful leaders to its walls. Only Sam Houston, greatest of the Texan great, resisted its magnetic appeal. Perhaps providentially, he organized the fight for freedom elsewhere. But he did not ignore the Alamo thrall. He gave his men at San Jacinto their "grito," their battle-cry, "Remember the Alamo! Remember Goliad!"

They have remained remembered. The Alamo has joined the national repertory of landmarks in the Westward Movement of the American people of the United States. However wrong, objectively, the phrase "Manifest Destiny" may be, the Alamo is a part of its meaning.

Historically, the Alamo embodies all four stages of New World expansion: discovery, conquest, colonization, independence. Only the last stage is absent from the Spanish history of the mission, deleted by the actions of President-General Santa Anna.

The success of the Americans and the failure of the Spanish in that part of New Spain now within our borders is often symbolized by historians in the Alamo. Reasons for the success were partly geographical, since Texas and California were so remote from the center of rule in Mexico. But the primary reason was the pattern of rule.

Rule rather than colonization was the Spanish purpose in coming to the New World. The rule was shaped by a system of mercantilism that required the raw materials of the colonies for support of Spanish wealth at home. Spain alone would monopolize all production, manufacturing, and distribution. Control from such a distance required an elaborate system, converting new Spain, and thereby Texas, into a controlled frontier. In contrast—by good luck, or perhaps sheer lawlessness—the American frontier was uncontrolled. And, in one sense, it was uncontrollable, so long as it remained frontier in the literal sense.

An example is the refusal of Americans to recognize the boundary of Texas as the Sabine River rather than the Rio Grande, although the 1819 Treaty with Spain declared the boundary publicly and officially. Americans pushed on past the Sabine into Texas.

There is not only humor but poetic truth in the story of the Tennessee lad who set out on his horse to join the fighting at the Alamo. When his neighbors, seeing his preparations for departure, wanted to know why he was leaving them, he said simply, "Why, I'm going to Texas to fight for my rights."

By "his rights," he meant vaguely yet accurately that men everywhere had the right to resist despotism and dictatorship; he meant the right to experience life as he and most Americans had experienced it; that is, the right to determine and create one's own destiny. In this profound sense, the Alamo is not merely "The Cradle of Texas Liberty" but "A Cradle of Liberty."

From its fall, from its defeat, it rose from those ashes to be a symbol of ultimate victory. Santa Anna's success at the siege of the Alamo was a Pyrrhic victory, one that cost more than it was worth.

The success of the Texas Revolution at San Jacinto, made possible by the self-sacrifice of the Texans at the Alamo, was the triumph of free men over an unworkable system. The Alamo will always be a tribute to the ultimate worth of the free individual, more precious than any "system."

But the system—until it came into competition with the democratic revolution—had been a logical one and worked for several centuries in geographies other than that of Texas. The establishment of Texas missions and the first Spanish towns testify that the system did allow for creative achievement. But the Crown was looking for mineral wealth; Texas was good only for farming and ranching.

As is well known, the actual arrival of La Salle provided the political reason for establishment of the first Spanish missions in Texas, although the friars had long insisted their government set up missions to Christianize the "peaceful" Indians of Texas (some of them were).

La Salle's intrusion likewise caused the establishment of San Antonio, however indirectly.

The Indian camping site of Yanaguana at what later was called the San Antonio River, inspired enthusiasm and projects in all, nearly all, who passed by it. San Antonio, like the Alamo itself, was a field of magnetic attraction.

The first *entrada* to succeed in finding La Salle's abandoned fort in 1689 was headed by Captain Alonso de León and Father Damián Manzanet, who had already an acquaintance with the Tejas Indians. Because La Salle's French colony was exterminated by disease and bad luck and hostile Karankawa Indians before de León ever found it, the French threat to Spain's ownership of Texas had evaporated.

Nonetheless, in 1691 Father Manzanet got to establish several missions in East Texas (all of which collapsed within two years). He came with Texas' first Governor, Domingo de Terán. They stopped on the way at Yanaguana, delighted with it, on June 13, St. Anthony's Day. Each wrote in his diary, "I named it San Antonio de Padua." Terán recommended the site for a pueblo, Fr. Manzanet for a mission.

The founding of San Antonio, and simultaneously of the mission that became known as the Alamo, had to wait three decades. Meantime, other Spaniards of power—the Marqués de Aguayo, Father Olivares, the great Father Margil—called attention of authorities to the vast promise for colonization of the San Antonio area—so wonderfully watered, so great and alluring, so beloved of the Indians.

It was none of these men, however, who primarily caused the ultimate establishment. It was another Frenchman, this time the romantic, pragmatic, enigmatic slippery trader from Nacogdoches, Saint Denis. Moving across Texas, unintercepted, in 1714 from that Louisiana northwestern outpost on down to the Rio Grande, this French adventurer (apparently out to increase profitable trade) alarmed Spanish officialdom again. And again, military leaders set out from the Rio Grande to establish Spanish claims bordering Louisiana by the traditional system: mission, pueblo constituted of baptized Indians converted both to Christianity and Spanish citizenry, and presidio or fort.

Saint Denis marveled at what a perfect townsite the San Antonio area represented; so did his friendly captor, Domingo Ramón (Saint Denis had married his captor's granddaughter); so did Fathers Hidalgo and Espinosa, already familiar with the region.

It would be a nearly central point, a "halfway-house," connecting the new missions in East Texas, the border missions at that time, with the several well-established missions along the Rio Grande, of which the supreme one was at Fort San Juan Bautista.

There was in fact a mission near San Juan Bautista which was really too close to two others. This was the mission beloved of Father Antonio Olivares, the Mission San Francisco Solano. It had been moved twice, closer to the Rio Grande, and it was to be moved northward again—and again, and again.

In 1718, the year that New Orleans was founded, the mission San Francisco Solano was transferred from the banks of the Rio Grande to the neighborhood of the San Pedro Springs, a transfer about 150 miles northward. This was the mission that was to become the mission San Antonio de Valero and later known as the Alamo. Its first site was not the one we now know, nor was its second.

If Saint Denis' journey across Texas provoked the Spanish answer of more missions, the immediate cause for the first mission at San Antonio was the remarkable Fransiscan father, Antonio de San Buenaventura Olivares.

Father Olivares, of the College of Queretaro, came to the Rio Grande border in 1699 to take part in the now vanished but once nearly magnificent mission cluster at San Juan Bautista, a score or so miles below present-day Eagle Pass. This nearly forgotten mission establishment on the Mexican side of the river had its days of considerable glory.

This cluster came into being after the failure of the far-off East Texas establishments in 1693. For decades it remained the gateway from conquered Mexico to the barbaric and unknown Spanish possession of Texas, and it was the training ground for Fray Olivares. There he learned Indian dialect, learned the mission techniques of teaching the Indian men how to plow and the women how to tend the crops, how to punish the wayward, how to lure runaways back with gifts of Mexican tobacco. But Father Olivares felt the pull of San Antonio.

In 1709 he secured permission, at royal expense, as always in the case of mission establishment, to conduct an inquiry north of the border in regard to possible locations. He was accompanied by a fellow Queretarian friar, Father Isídro Félix de Espinosa, and by Captain Pedro de Aguirre with fourteen soldiers. The group arrived at San Pedro Springs or its creek (giving it that name themselves) on April 8. They, too, named the river "San Antonio de Padua." They continued east as far as the Colorado but turned back on April 19 after failing to find, as Father Olivares hoped, any Tejas Indians. The inspection tour yielded copious notes; on a trip to Spain that same year, Olivares presented them to the king.

At last, in 1716, after the disturbing 1714 arrival at Fort San Juan Bautista of Saint Denis, Father Olivares got authorization from the viceroy to set up a mission at San Pedro Springs. Father Olivares had to wait a year at the missions on the Rio Grande before the expedition was finally ordered. The governmental chief was Don Martín de Alarcón, who was to push on to East Texas to investigate conditions there and to check on French intrusion into Texas.

The departure of the San Antonio founders in 1718 from Fort San Juan Bautista was not auspicious. Father Olivares found the new governor and captain-general of Texas, Don Martín de Alarcón, terribly slow. But Alarcón had problems of recruitment, and the Indians around were rebellious. The two men grew acrimonious. When the expedition was at last ready to cross the ford on April 9, 1718, Alarcón crossed without Fr. Olivares, who, angrily refusing to travel with Alarcón, left nine days later, with a few of his Indian converts at San Francisco Solano, to serve as interpreters. They followed different routes to meet May 1 at San Pedro Springs. Father Espinosa set out from East Texas to meet the expedition in San Antonio.

Alarcón was a Spanish soldier of fortune with a signal career back of him. He became governor of the Province of Coahuila in 1705, then governor of the Province of Texas in 1716. He is usually called the founder of the city of San Antonio. His expedition set out in April, consisting of seventy-two persons, including seven families who were to become inhabitants of the new pueblo accompanying Father Olivares' mission.

The mission, a temporary site, was founded on May 1 with appropriate ceremony near the springs; the town of Villa de Bexar, named after the famous duke and brother of the viceroy, was founded on May 5. Alarcón went on to East Texas, after a return trip to the Rio Grande to secure more provisions for the new village of Bexar, and he did not return to San Antonio until February, 1719. Six months later he was relieved of the governorship of the province. Meantime, Father Olivares also made a trip to East Texas to get some good carpenters. When he brought back two French carpenters from Louisiana, Governor Alarcón would not let them stay on Spanish soil.

In time, San Antonio would replace San Juan Bautista as gateway to the adventure of colonizing Texas. The imposing Franciscan architecture of San Bernardo would be surpassed by the glory of San Antonio's San José—though never rivaled by the Alamo's architecture.

The Alamo, as was the custom in the Spanish system for missions, was intended to be merely the opening and transient stage in the founding of a new community, Christianized and civilized by European standards. It was merely a seed-pueblo from which the community would grow. In this initial stage, it was to be self-sufficient, save for the presidio (or the few soldiers living at the mission to protect the experiment from hostile Indians). Its primary work was in no sense that of a seminary.

The mission building followed a set pattern, four thick and solid protective walls surrounding the house for the two or three missionaries, the quarters for the Indians, the granary, the workrooms, the cemetery, and the church.

Outside the mission were its fields for cultivation, sometimes its orchard though this often was inside the enclosed quadrangle, and beyond the fields were the ranches.

It was beautifully planned, and it had worked extremely well in Mexico. But the Indians of Texas were far less advanced than their Aztec neighbors. They found domestication difficult. Above all, unlike the Aztecs, they had no highly developed, formalized religion for which Christianity could be substituted. They were nomads. They could not protect crown lands from the wilder, predatory Indians. They did not want to be farmers. The burden of the Texas friars was sharply different from that of the Franciscans in Mexico.

The good fathers were not unaware of their special problem in Texas. But miracles had happened in Mexico and they might happen here, despite the isolation and remoteness from power in the great center of the New World, Mexico City.

The Alarcón-Olivares colony is usually regarded as the first Spanish settlement in what was then thought of as Texas (El Paso and its neighboring settlements were part of the New Mexico colonizing).

The site, like that of Texas itself, has had a puzzling confusion of names. In 1691, Father Manzanet had named the Indian village, Yanaguana, on the river, San Antonio de Padua. In 1709, the expedition of Fathers Olivares and Espinosa named either a creek or its springs San Pedro (*Agua de San Pedro*) and called the river "San Antonio de Padua." Alarcón called his hamlet Villa de Bexar, his presidio, San Antonio de Bexar, and the mission, San Antonio de Valero. The town would later, in 1731, be named San Fernando de Bexar. The name, San Antonio, prevailed in time.

One witness of the official founding ceremonies in 1718 is worth noting. He was the original Payaya Indian chief who had received Father Manzanet at Yanaguana in 1691.

The mission which Father Olivares had originally called San Antonio de Padua was the first Querétarian mission in Texas. Of the twenty or more Indian tribes around, the first ones to whom Father Olivares ministered were the Payayas, Sanas and Pampoas. He had brought from San Francisco Solano several Jarami Indians trained there and who were no doubt of great help as interpreters, for the Indians of this area spoke their tribal dialects plus a sort of *lingua franca*, or all-purpose tongue, known as Coahuiltecan.

The first temporary structures for Father Olivares' mission were on the west side of the river, indeed, west of San Pedro Creek. In late 1718 or early 1719, Father Olivares moved the mission to the east bank of the river where the land was more desirable and the irrigation easier.

A terrible hurricane in 1724 demolished this mission's *jacales* for the Indians, and the mission was moved again, this time only "two gun-shots distance" from the earlier site. The move was completed by 1727, to the spot where the present Alamo stands. Some historians believe there was first the site on the west bank, then two on the east. Adding the two locations of San Francisco Solano on the Rio Grande, the present site would represent the fifth location of the mission that became the Alamo.

Indeed, it had a rough time so far as "permanency" is concerned. The major chapel, begun in 1744, designed with an ornamental front and two towers, collapsed twelve years later. The chapel or church which we now know as the Alamo was begun in 1758.

Survival for the Alamo has been a career. At the

time of the last re-location in 1727, the Alamo had as missioners seventy families of Indians from three tribes. Considering the Indian tendency to run away and the hankering for the old ways, this was a respectable showing. The abortive mission effort of San Francisco Xavier Najera was added to it about this time.

Most of the early work consisted of setting up housing and ditching the water from the river to irrigate the fields. Religious services were first held in a hut.

Raiding Apaches and an epidemic of cholera, which also struck neighboring San Jose in 1738, decreased the Indian population of the Alamo to 184. Undaunted, the fathers recruited new converts and raised the population to 261 just four years before the cornerstone for the new chapel was laid in 1744 under the administration of Father Mariano Francisco de los Dolores.

Building flourished henceforth. A 1745 report describes two rows of adobe houses within the quadrangle walls, separated by a water ditch; the monastery, where the missionaries lived, three cells on the second story; the completed weaving room where clothes and blankets were made from locally produced cotton and wool.

The tower of the new church was completed in 1761. The sacristy roof had caved in, alas, because of inexperienced workers, but it was being rebuilt. As for the convent, it was completed with arcaded cloisters on both ground and second floors. The kitchen, the portero, refectory, and offices were in fine shape and religiously decorated. Seven houses were now made of stone, with arched *portales*. Willows and fruit trees grew along the *acequia* or water ditch in the quadrangle plaza. A well had been dug and properly curbed with stone. The outer walls were high and thick for protection from Indian raids; a tower rose over the main entrance to the plaza.

This cooperative commonwealth was nearly self-sufficient. It had a population of 275 in 1762. Among these, as the Franciscans noted with pride, were 32 Karankawas from the coast, a warlike—perhaps cannibalistic—tribe in dire need of civilizing.

There exists a fascinating official description of the Alamo mission as it was in 1762, although this document contains—according to the Bureau of American Ethnology in its *Handbook of American Indians*—an "obvious exaggeration" of the number of converted Indians.

The document begins: "In this province are some beautiful springs. So great is the volume of water which they send forth, that within a short distance a river of considerable size is formed. . . . Across the river on its eastern bank and about two gunshots from the presidio is the mission of San Antonio de Valero. . . . The records show that since its foundation seventeen hundred and ninety-two persons have been baptized. At present there are seventy-six families here, which counting widows and widowers, orphans and other children, comprises two hundred and seventy-five persons."

The convent is described as nearly fifty yards square, "with arcades above and below." The convent contains not only the living quarters of the religious, but also the porter's lodge, the dining room, the kitchen and offices. "All these rooms are adorned with sacred ornaments . . ."

In the second court, there is a room "large enough for four looms," and on these looms the Indians make a coarse cloth used in clothes, shawls and blankets. In two neighboring rooms are kept the stock of wool, cotton, combs, skeins, spindles, cards and other items required for the making of clothes.

"The church," the report says, "of this mission was finished, even to the towers and the sacristy, but, on account of the stupidity of the builder, it tumbled down. Another, however, of pleasing architecture, is being constructed of hewn stones. For the present a room which was built for a granary serves as church."

In addition to an altar and a wooden table, this room had a sculptured image of St. Anthony, in a niche; one of St. John, and an image of Christ crucified. All of

these, the report says somewhat bafflingly, were dressed in "robes, undergarments and silken vestments."

The inventory of the sacristy—"a big room"—states
that large boxes contain the ornaments; among these,
and all in silver, were three covered chalices, two large
cups, four communion vessels, a silken case for the
cross, a vessel and a sprinkler for holy water, two can-
dlesticks, an incense boat and spoon, a censer and three
holy oil vials.

And: "The mission has a well-built stone chapel,
eleven yards long. Among its ornaments is a stone
cross two yards high and capped with silver. In the
cross are four hidden reliquaries, each containing its
own relic. The altar is adorned with carved and painted images."

The inventory of practical equipment is impressive:
The Indian dwellings are furnished with "high beds,
chests, metates, pots, flat earthen pans, kettles, caul-
drons and boilers." There are "seven rows of houses . . .
made of stone" (which must mean seven stone units in
a row). "With their arched porticoes, the houses form
a broad and beautiful plaza through which runs a canal
skirted by willows and fruit trees." Three cannon stand
guard over the main gate tower.

And, for cultivating the fields of "corn, chile, and
beans that are tilled to feed the Indians, and of cotton
to clothe them, there are fifty pairs of cart oxen . . .
traces, plows, plowshares, fifty axes, forty pickaxes,
twenty-two crowbars and twenty-five sickles."

In addition there are twelve carts for general haul-
ing, carpenter tools such as adzes, chisels, planes, picks,
hammers, saws, files, and also a forge.

The mission ranch included a stone house, twenty-
five yards long, porticoed and divided into three rooms,
these occupied by families watching after the stock.
The stock included—impressively enough—"one hundred and fifteen gentle horses, one thousand one hundred and fifteen head of cattle, two thousand three hundred sheep and goats, two hundred mares, fifteen jen-

nies and eighteen saddle mules." (Tempting indeed for the Comanche and Apache raiders.)

Still, all might have gone well with the Alamo had it not been for its neighboring royal villa. The growing town became a rival, a rival for the mission land primarily which was close enough to be protected from the predatory Apaches and Comanches.

San Antonio was having growing pains.

In 1731, a great and promising event occurred for the city of San Antonio. The fathers got a new town, the first officially recognized civil settlement in Texas, having its own municipal government. The king himself, besought by the Marques de Aguayo, arranged for the new community, offering enticing advantages to Canary Islanders who would volunteer to move to Texas and found there a new life.

This action was the result of the long-time plea of the mission fathers to the central government to send in settlers from Mexico or Spain who would show the Indian converts how to live in a civilized community. True. there were Mexican families in the town, but mostly these were the families of the soldiers, and the soldiers were too often forced into service from the most shiftless classes, not to mention the jails.

Fifty-six Canary Islanders, representing a total of sixteen families, accepted the offer, with the agreement the government would pay transportation, maintenance for one year, and give them treatment as aristocrats, bestowing the title "Hidalgo" on the men, and offering land and water, and pasture benefits. They were to endow San Antonio with some of its most famous families.

After a harrowing journey by sea and land, they arrived at 11 o'clock on the morning of March 9, 1731. They had with them elaborate governmental directions for establishing a fine settlement; streets laid off, sites for a Main Plaza and a church, priests' houses, land assignments. The land assignments were north and northwest—lands the missions had not taken.

Unfortunately, the plan interfered with Apache habits. Outlying pastures, fields, and ranches were under Apache dominion. The Canary Islanders were soon at odds with both the religious and the military. They wanted to live like royalty, as some Spaniards and Creoles did in the scattered haciendas they saw on their long journey up from Veracruz port into the wilderness.

They spurned manual labor, spurned the miserable settlement south of the Alamo known as La Villita. They wanted the mission Indians as slaves to work their fields. They wanted some of the mission lands; they wanted water for irrigation in competition with mission needs.

They loved litigation, and they resisted any levies on their money or energy. In 1772, for example, the Governor Ripperdá tried to execute a plan agreed on the year before to rebuild the barracks of the garrison stationed at San Antonio, as a further help in fending off Indian raids. The Islanders lodged an official protest against the insistence that they help in the work, asserting that as land-owners it was not part of their duty to perform the tasks of soldiers and their families. They bitterly fought the missions in competition over supplying food and goods for the presidio trade.

They were not a great help in setting an example of the kind of life for which the Indian was being trained at the mission, and neither were the members of the military.

In 1737, Father Dolores of the Alamo Mission ordered the destruction of the bridge over the river, since he did not care "to have the troublesome military attend mass in his chapel." This was an offense to the dignity of Governor Franquís' power and office. Outraged, he ordered it rebuilt. Arriving to inspect the new bridge, he was intercepted by an Indian stationed there by Father Dolores to inform the governor he was forbidden to cross the mission property. The governor crossed.

At intervals, the fathers also vetoed attendance at mass in their chapel of the Canary Islanders. But, in 1745, only the arrival of 100 Indians from the Alamo to help in a crisis saved the town's fight against an Apache attack.

Conflicts and changes continued as Texas began to be settled. The missions were secularized in 1793 and the official reason given was that the Indian should be given his full rights as subject of the Spanish king. But the fundamental reason was really that Spain's purse was nearly empty from supporting with royal subsidy missions that were not self-sufficient. Royal Spain was enfeebled, its dominant role in the world nearing its end. The mission chapels were to become parish churches, supported by the local population.

By a royal cedula of 1773, the missions in East Texas were evacuated, for Spain had acquired Louisiana; the struggling and weak East Texas missions were no longer needed as symbolic frontier forts or villages. Most of the surrounding settlers moved to San Antonio later and were allotted secularized land of the San Antonio de Valero mission. Officially the San Antonio mission was secularized at the same time, but continued its own distinct existence, apart from the town, for another ten years.

Its school was finally closed in either 1783 or 1785. The last baptism was recorded in 1783; the last marriage was recorded in 1785. Secularization was completed by 1794. The records of the mission were transferred to the curacy of Bexar; or, the San Fernando church. The Alamo thus lacked twenty-four years serving an entire century as a mission, but its significant life was not over.

The inventory at the time of transfer of its archives to San Fernando parish is revealing. The convent was one square of stone and adobe walls, about 75 yards long and 75 yards wide. The west and north sides of the convent were two storeys high, "with six corridors, and five rooms which served as cells," fifteen feet wide and twelve feet high. The roof leaked and otherwise needed repair.

The north-south surrounding wall of the plaza of

the mission was 175 varas long; the east-west dimension was 58 varas. The walls were three-quarters of a vara thick and three varas high, constructed of stone, adobe, and mud. The principal entrance was in the south wall, which was fifty varas wide and four varas high. The granary was in bad condition; it was thirty varas long, adobe floored, and united the house of the padres to the dwellings of the Indians, which were in the square of the Arcades in the western part. Only twelve of these were usable; the rest was in ruins.

The church had never been finished. Its workmanship was described as "crude." The principal doorway, however, was called "beautiful, and of Tuscan workmanship." The baptistry was finished except for wooden doors. Only the presbytery had its tower arch. Of the four niches on the facade for nearly life-size statues, only two were ornamented with stone images— San Francisco and Santo Domingo. The columns for the upper two niches had not been put in place. The stone cornice was lacking.

As the inventory noted, all the roofs needed repair, if they were not to fall in ruins.

Despite the secularization, there were still 139 people living in the Alamo "pueblo," according to the census of 1797. A few years later, in 1803, the Alamo mission became a barracks.

To protect the town from Indians, the Flying Company (mounted troops) of San Carlo de Parras was stationed in San Antonio. Its home pueblo back in Mexico was known as San Jose y Santiago del Alamo de Parras. These soldiers set up barracks along the south side of the mission San Antonio de Valero and used the rooms inside the walls. The church became a military chapel. Soon the company's records referred to its location as the "Pueblo del Alamo," and soon the mission became known as the Alamo. Some historians insist, however, that the name derives from the cottonwood trees (los alamos) so thick in this region. The Flying Company operated in and out of the Alamo, at intervals, until the late 1820's.

But it was not the destiny of the Alamo to pass simply from mission to fort. It also served briefly as a hospital, probably the first hospital in San Antonio. This service began in 1806 when the compound was designated a military hospital for soldiers of all the Spanish eastern provinces. In time it served the citizens of San Antonio as well. The first staff included one doctor, one orderly, and one male nurse. There were 42 patients in the first year suffering from "chronic illnesses." The hospital provided good medical treatment for the people, and its program of vaccination (supplied free to those unable to pay) helped halt the frequent smallpox epidemics in early-day San Antonio. The epidemics between 1778 and 1781 nearly killed off the mission Indian population.

In 1813, the Alamo had its first, but not last, occupation by Americans. Not as mission, not as hospital, but as fortress.

The Americans were soldiers of fortune, allied with Father Hidalgo's first abortive attempt to liberate Mexico from Spain. Influenced by one of Hidalgo's surviving lieutenants, Bernardo Gutierrez—who had escaped to the States—Lieutenant Augustus Magee of the American army in Louisiana organized American "freebooters" to join Gutierrez in establishing an independent republic in Texas. It was a wild, romantic scheme that had at first an extraordinary success. The City of San Antonio surrendered on April 1, 1813; the revolutionaries quickly declared the first "Republic of Texas."

The American army made its headquarters in the Alamo. But the triumph—like the idealism—was very short-lived. Brilliantly repelling one attack of the Spanish government, which had mustered 3,000 men under General Elizondo, in July, the new republicans fell to quarrelling among themselves over the spoils. The American leaders were especially astounded at the brutality of the revenge the Mexican leaders inflicted upon their captured fellow-countrymen.

When Spain returned to the attack at the end of July under the ruthlessly capable General Arredondo, the hotheads were gulled into a trap and rapidly destroyed. Arredondo lured them outside the city, and no fighting took place in town or at the Alamo. Spanish rule and royalism were saved for a while.

But Mexico City caught a glimpse of a new potential enemy, the westward-yearning Anglo-Americans. There had been minor "intrusions" before, such as that of Philip Nolan in 1800 under pretext of hunting wild horses. It had been quickly crushed. But the Augustus Magee-Bernardo Gutierrez try was real and nearly full-scale invasion. And it might have had a different outcome if restless American soldiery had not been fully engaged in the 1812 War with Great Britain.

The Flying Company of Parras, which had abandoned its Alamo location during the incipient revolution, soon returned. From now on, the mission's history would be that of a fort.

But it assumed a new function as a prison when Arredondo visited his inhuman vengefulness on the town of San Antonio. Because uprisings had occurred in the city in favor of Hidalgo's revolution, Arredondo marched his army into town on August 20 to make the city pay.

The Alamo plaza was converted into a sort of outdoor *carcel,* or prison pen. Arredondo's aides rounded up 800 prisoners of every social station, including battle captives. Those captured with weapons upon them were immediately executed—not at the Alamo but on Military Plaza. The executions, with Arredondo serving as sole and relentless tribunal, were halted at sunset, to resume in the morning. Three hundred citizens accused of sympathy with the revolution were stacked into an airless granary to spend the night. Of those who did not suffocate during the night, most were shot by next noonday. Executions continued as a daily occurrence until summer's end. Then the Alamo ceased to be a *carcel*.

There was not much population left in San Antonio after the vindicative retribution of Arredondo for the 1813 revolution. A young officer in Arredondo's retinue absorbed the chief's methods carefully. He would return again, practiced in revenge. He was Antonio López de Santa Anna.

After the executions of 1813 and San Antonio's "Noche Triste" of August 20, the place was for a few years "almost entirely abandoned," according to one report. But when Mexico won its revolution and independence in 1821, the emigrants returned, and the town soon had a population of around 4,000. Mexico was in such turmoil, such struggle for power, no one there would pay much attention for a time to remote Texas.

Land-hungry people elsewhere did. The Americans had been paying much attention to Texas ever since the Louisiana Purchase, and numerous "squatters" had crossed the border illegally to settle in East Texas. With the empresario arrangement set up by Moses Austin and his son, Stephen, in 1821, the intrusion became legal. And Texas was, compared to the Spanish achievement, rapidly settled. By 1835, there were perhaps 30,000 Anglo-Americans living in Texas as Mexican citizens, and their communities were thriving. By 1836 they had established another "Republic of Texas." In this achievement the Alamo mission played its most historic role.

There is no need here to summarize the causes and the growth of the Texas revolution. In essence, it finally resolved into a conflict between the American colonists who insisted on self-government in one way or another and the Mexican dictator, President-General Santa Anna who was in no mood for compromise, and who had betrayed, as the colonists felt, the spirit of the Mexican War of Independence from Spain.

The rebellious spirit of the colonists, thwarted by Mexican laws in fully developing their land or state, grew from early smoulderings in 1830 into a blaze in late 1835. The "Anglo" leaders—Stephen F. Austin, Sam Houston, James Bowie, William Barret Travis, others—all knew Santa Anna had to be opposed, although they were terribly split about how.

The galvanizing event occurred in September of 1835. Santa Anna sent his brother-in-law, General Martin Perfecto de Cós, with an army to San Antonio for two purposes: (1) to capture certain Texas rebels, such as Travis, and (2) to subdue the population. There would be no reasonable discussion of differences or problems—such as taxes and custom duties and the establishing of schools, and reforms in the judicial system. There would be only a show of power and imperious domination.

The Texans knew what kind of treatment they could expect. They weren't defending their lands. They were defending their lives.

So, they organized, electing Austin their commander-in-chief, although he was the least warlike of men, and marched on San Antonio. Austin's purpose was to make Cós listen to reason; the army enthusiastically proposed to throw him out of Texas. Austin thought of the aftermath, but they did not. This difference in aim was no problem after the provisional government voted to send Austin to the United States to get help in the shape of men, money, and ammunition.

Stalled at first by Austin in their camp at Mission Concepcíon (where they brilliantly defeated an attack by Cós). they were liberated by Austin's departure. When Ben Milam yelled, "Who will go with Ol' Ben Milam into Bexar?" they whooped and hollered. But they had the good sense to make careful plans first.

General Cós had a thousand men garrisoned at the Alamo. Anticipating trouble, he had carefully barricaded the town, cut down trees, fortified the plaza, deployed cannon on top San Fernando church, placed snipers on roof tops. Half his men were stationed in town.

The Texans had maps of Cós' defenses, supplied by

Anglo residents in the town, Samuel Maverick and John W. ("Colorado") Smith. Their strategy was to make a feint on the Alamo, drawing off the troops in town and then to hurl their main strength at the undefended (they hoped) city.

The attack broke on December 5 with wild gunfire in the town plaza. As the Texans advanced from house to house, some of Cós' officers began to walk out on him. He ordered all his troops into the Alamo, a half-mile east and across the San Antonio River from the two plazas on either side of the town's San Fernando church. Poor old Ben Milam was one of two Texas casualties, killed by a sniper on the second day of battle.

To the Texans' surprise, Cós surrendered on the fourth day. Part of the credit was deserved by the leaders of San Antonio, Mexicans, who wanted separate statehood as much perhaps as the Texans, who offered very few supplies to Cós, and who demoralized Cós' army, destroying its will to fight.

Cós demanded the right to keep his artillery and supplies and wanted the Texans to fire a salute as he moved his troops out of the Alamo. He lost. The terms were severe. He had to swear never to take up arms above the Rio Grande again. He had to leave fourteen cannon in the Alamo, along with stores and supplies, a veritable fortune for the Texans. And he had left another valuable contribution; he put the Alamo into some shape as a fort.

Once again the Texans had triumphantly driven the armed forces of Mexico out of their state. They thought the war was over, and, just as in 1832, they got over-confident. Most of the volunteers went home to tend to spring planting. The youngsters and adventurers from the states who didn't yet own land grants like the settlers stayed on in San Antonio. It was the only "city" between New Orleans and Santa Fe.

Shortly, Governor Smith and his Council—the two agencies of the provisional Texas government—were at each other's throats. The Council threatened to impeach him, then did declare him removed from office. He said they were crazy, unconstitutional and stupid and wouldn't get out. They wouldn't give in. Texas, which had apparently just won its fight for statehood, now had two rival governments, even with Santa Anna out of the running.

Sam Houston warned that Santa Anna would try for revenge soon, and he warned the Texans of the insanity of fighting among themselves. He threw his power on the side of Governor Smith. The Council, responding with childish anger, got even by naming Fannin supreme commander. Fannin was now busy with 500 young recruits—mostly from Georgia—working as laborers to convert Goliad into a gleaming toy of a fort.

Two other Texans decided they might as well take over and lead the Texas army. Francis Johnson, who succeeded Ben Milam after his death, took most of the volunteers at San Antonio into the camp of a brilliant Scottish doctor, James Grant. Dr. Grant, wounded while fighting bravely at San Antonio, wanted to invade Mexico. He owned a vast plantation in Coahuila which Santa Anna's followers had confiscated. He raised again the dream of a great Southwestern Empire that had haunted many Americans and ruined Aaron Burr. The wealth of Mexico is ours to take, Dr. Grant urged. He wanted to take the Port of Matamoras, insisted a great army of Mexican volunteers awaiting Texan leadership would rebel against Santa Anna.

Sam Houston was not going to let the Texan army be stolen from his command without a fight. He rallied his friends: Bowie, Travis, Fannin. On the chance the Mexican venture might pan out, Houston ordered Bowie to muster a company and beat the Grant-Johnson expedition to the Mexican border. He got Fannin, who decided to take his Goliad men on the Matamoros gold rush, to change his mind and stay put at the sparkling fort, now named Fort Defiance.

Bowie missed his message, so Houston then ordered him to go to the Alamo, recommending that he blow it up so Santa Anna couldn't use it when he came. He told Bowie to haul off the artillery to Gonzales or to Fannin at nearby Goliad.

All this time, Houston was trying to handle the daily squabbles between impeached Governor Smith and the firebrands of the Council.

The Texans now realistically anticipated an attempt from General Santa Anna to avenge Cós' defeat and believed he would come sometime after mid-March when the unpredictable winter and "blue northers" had passed.

They underestimated him. Even though he had to move an army over uninhabited near-desert for 300 miles between San Antonio and the capital of Coahuila, an advance wing reached the Rio Grande by Christmas day.

Although Santa Anna had emptied the jails of northern Mexico to swell his army to 7,000 or so men, he had brilliant officers, some being veterans of European wars and trained by Napoleon, or in the royal army of Spain. The General, himself, was coached in warfare by Napoleonic veterans and referred to himself as "The Napoleon of the West." His practical experience in uses of violence and terrorism were learned under General Arredondo in San Antonio in 1813.

With Santa Anna, reluctantly, was the bedraggled Cós who had the bad luck to encounter the Mexican army in his retreat and was ordered to start back to reconquer San Antonio and the Alamo.

Like a magnet, the Alamo continued to draw men to it. Although Sam Houston recommended to three men, Bowie, Travis, and Neill, that they blow it up and move its cannon into the Anglo settlements, all three agreed it would be wrong. They considered the Alamo the key to the defense of Texas. If Santa Anna captured it, he would have the strongest fort in the state. From it, he could resist attack and send out squadrons to destroy, one by one, the score of American settlements, all lying east of the Alamo. From the West, he would have an uncontested supply line. Early in February, Bowie wrote Governor Smith: "Colonel Neill and myself have come to the solemn resolution that we will rather die in these ditches than give them up to the enemy."

On the day that letter was dispatched, William Barret Travis arrived at the Alamo with a detachment of 25 men, ordered by Governor Smith to blow up the Alamo. Travis could only concur with Bowie and Neill—to destroy the Alamo would be a great blunder.

So the old mission which was now a fort was still standing February 8 when that extraordinary man—nationally famous frontiersman, former congressman from Tennessee, more a legendary figure than Jim Bowie—David Crockett, arrived to fight with the Texans. On the day Crockett arrived in San Antonio with a dozen friends, Santa Anna's main army reached the Rio Grande, 150 miles below the Alamo. Gradually, all the actors in the great drama were coming together. Only Sam Houston moved out of the Alamo's magic radius. Disgusted with the squabbling between the two rival sides of the Texas government, he asked Governor Smith for a furlough to go off and make sure the 2,000 Cherokee Indians around Nacogdoches would not ally with the Mexican side.

Houston was still a general, but he had no soldiers to command. He counted on the convention meeting March 1 to create order in the Texas chaos and was confident his army would be returned to him at this meeting. He did not believe Santa Anna would enter Texas until the middle of March.

Friendly Mexicans in San Antonio kept warning the Texans that Santa Anna was at the border or nearby—a baker at Laredo notified San Antonio friends he had got huge orders to bake bread and have it ready for the army at once. But the Texans were fighting among themselves for the top army posts and paid little attention.

With the false sense of security from the defeat of

Cós, they plunged into a welcome celebration in San Antonio for Davy Crockett that outdid the one he received in Nacogdoches. David responded with a speech, exhibited his famous rifle, "Old Betsy" and played his fiddle, accompanied by a Scot named McGregor, on the bagpipes.

Everyone danced in the plaza and few men turned up next morning for the daily drill. But the biggest celebration was to honor George Washington's birthday, February 22. Davy made another speech. Davy's father had fought with the volunteers of Washington's first army, an army of unprofessional soldiers like this one in Texas. The Texans were well aware that their revolution was just like that of their forefathers under Washington's leadership. The Texans were resisting tyranny, absentee ownership, and taxation without representation. History, in the remote and sandy little town of San Antonio, was once again repeating itself. The same story, in a way, as that of the thirteen colonies.

There is one account, never proved, which claims that General Santa Anna, who unknown to the Texans had reached the outskirts of San Antonio the day before, took part in disguise in the fandango honoring *el senor* Jorge Washington. It is true that he reached the banks of the Medina, twenty miles away, on February 21 after a bitter and amazing march up from the Rio Grande. He might have surprised the Texans that night but for a flood that prevented crossing his artillery over the river.

But at least the Texans found out that night that Santa Anna's advance forces were encamped on the Medina River. A Mexican leader of the citizens of San Antonio who cast their lot with the Texans, Captain Juan Seguin of a fine old family, summoned Bowie and Travis at the dance and gave them the news. They decided to post a sentry at dawn on the roof of San Fernando. A sudden shower brought the fandango to a close.

The rain stopped during the night. The young sentry was cold in the bell terror. He stamped his feet to keep warm, blew on his hands and looked to the west for signs of life. None. It was a bare and empty land without movement. To the south and west, the mesquite thickets covered the flat land. Northwest and north the horizon was cut by pleasant hills, as it was on the east.

A half-mile east of the church, the sentry could see the morning sun caught within the shadows of the Alamo walls, the adobe and stone of the fort a mellow and pleasing sandy grey. It drowsed in the sun just east of the big horseshoe bend of the clear-flowing San Antonio River.

From the sentry's post across the river, the Alamo looked like a walled, rectangular plaza, the long part north and south like a football field and just about the same dimensions, 150 yards by 56 yards. The walls of the rectangle housed flat-roofed adobe-brick rooms on the south and west sides. On the east the same rooms, except that the middle part was two-storeys high, what had been the convent of the mission. The church or chapel, which is all that people think of today when they think of the Alamo, was set back some fifty feet at the southeast corner of the plaza rectangle, thus having its own little court in front of it. Looking from the sentry's post, then, the open space between walls made an L-shaped plaza. The walls were generally thick, about three feet, and about nine feet high. The two-storey convent and the chapel ran their walls up to about twenty feet.

North of the Alamo chapel, east of the two-storey convent structure, there were enclosed areas for gardening and storage, and a cattle pen. The chapel had no wall connecting its south side with the south wall of the plaza rectangle. The Texans had closed this breach by setting up a stockade fence, double rows of stout posts filled in with hard-packed earth to absorb cannon balls. Jim Bowie and Engineer Green Jameson worked hard getting the Alamo ready, with ramps of dirt and timber spaced inside the plaza for the cannon General Cós had reluctantly left. There were also cannon platforms inside the chapel at either end, which Cós had erected.

The musing sentry wondered why a clatter of carts loaded with household possessions was frantically moving in the streets leading north of town with what seemed the entire Mexican population behind them.

Then, the sentry lifted his eyes and sighted the west again. The breath went out of him and he couldn't stir. There on the Alizan heights, hundreds, maybe thousands, of Mexican lancers, with shining helmets and weapons, were filling the emptiness he had seen there before. Panic nearly got him. He grabbed the bell rope and pulled with all his might. The mighty peals brought Travis and Dr. Sutherland from the square below on a run up the rickety wood stairs.

Since the bell had also warned away the Mexicans at drill, Travis saw nothing. Maybe fear had duped the sentry. Dr. Sutherland and John W. Smith volunteered to get on their horses and ride out to the western hills to scout. "Watch us," Sutherland told Travis, "if we come racing back, you'll know what to do."

The young doctor and the San Antonio businessman reached a gentle rise about a mile and a half out of town. They looked down in a hidden valley on the troops at drill. Breathless, they wheeled around and whipped their ponies to a breakneck speed, praying they had not been seen by the Mexicans. Dr. Sutherland's mount stumbled and fell on the road still slippery from last night's rain. Smith hurried back and helped him mount up, but Sutherland's spill had lamed him. They raced into town as the vindicated sentry pulled at the bell rope again with all his might.

Travis ordered the men into the Alamo. He needed 1,000 men. With only 150, it would be foolhardy to try to hold the town. The Alamo must be their refuge until help could come.

Luckily, Travis, who was sharing joint command

with the ailing Jim Bowie (a terribly sick man and mere shadow of his former self), had sent for help a few days ago. He had dispatched his boyhood friend, James Bonham of South Carolina, to bring Fannin from Goliad with his 500 men. Bonham was due back any moment.

Travis hastened to the Alamo, leaving Crockett to handle the retreat of the men. Though sick, Bowie had his wits about him. He detailed men to round up all the cattle in sight and drive them into the pens at the Alamo. He sent others to raid barns for grain. Thirty beeves went through the gates; 80 sacks of corn were lugged, carted, carried into the Alamo. They might eat nothing but beef and corn, but they wouldn't starve before help came. Fannin would have to come now.

General Santa Anna was on the move too. In brilliant regalia, he rode into the now empty town shortly after noon and took possession. He had about 2,500 troops. At least that many more were soon to swell his numbers.

He settled himself in the luxury he loved with wine in good supply, thinking the mere sight of his army had already scared the Texans into surrender. He ordered a message sent to the Texans, in Bowie's care, calling for unconditional surrender. Bowie, of course, rejected such terms, but he thought a parley might not do any harm. Bowie was said to own a million acres or more of Texas land. He had a lot to protect. He had dealt expertly with the Mexicans. But Travis didn't hesitate nor consult anyone else. In his long rivalry with Bowie, victory was now in his hands. Bowie was too sick to compete. Travis fired a cannon ball into the air. His answer was clear—and contemptuous. The only talk would be with gunfire.

Santa Anna replied in kind. Quickly, the Mexicans ran up a blood-red flag over San Fernando church. This was the signal of "no quarter"—win, or know you'll die. No mercy, no captives, no surrender was the ultimatum. For the losers, certain death down to the very last man.

Santa Anna could be patient. His fieldpieces, his

artillery, were mostly on the way. Other battalions were due. His men needed rest. He posted guards around the Alamo to close retreat exits. He stationed units on the roads around to intercept any other Texan troops coming to help. He was expert at the war of nerves. His bands blared at night to keep Texans from sleeping. The Mexicans could sleep in relays, but there were so few Texans, they had to be always on the alert and couldn't get any real sleep.

The Texans didn't mind, if aid were on the way. Initial reports were discouraging, for Jim Bonham rode through the gates on the first day, at dusk, chased by Mexicans, to report that Fannin didn't think he should leave Goliad. The Texans were certain, however, that when news of Santa Anna's surprise arrival reached Fannin, the answer would be different. The Texas convention was to meet at Washington-on-the-Brazos on March 1. Santa Anna started the siege on February 23. If help were not already on the way, it soon would be.

Davy Crockett picked off the first Mexican victim on the first day in a startling demonstration of long-range marksmanship. The Texans didn't lose a man that first day, nor for the next ten, according to the Travis letters to Houston and the government which his courier succeeded in getting through the Mexican lines.

The Texans were holding their fire, buying time, keeping Santa Anna occupied while Sam Houston put an army together. With Fannin's 400 or 500 core, it shouldn't take long. Meantime, the Texans used their sharpshooting skill to wreak havoc on Mexican attempts to move their camps ever nearer the walls. With great daring, they went out of the fort at night in sorties to burn the huts which gave the Mexican troops protection.

Travis wrote with the pride to the convention about his men. Few documents in American history match his famous statement, composed on the second day of the siege:

Commandancy of the Alamo
Bexar, F'by 24th, 1836

To the people of Texas & All Americans in the World:

Fellow Citizens and Compatriots—I am besieged by a thousand or more of the Mexicans under Santa Anna. I have sustained a continual Bombardment and cannonade for 24 hours and have not lost a man. The enemy has demanded a surrender at discretion, otherwise, the garrison are to be put to the sword, if the fort is taken. I have answered the demand with a cannon shot, and our flag still waves proudly from the walls. *I shall never surrender or retreat.* Then I call upon you in the name of liberty, of patriotism, and everything dear to the American character, to come to our aid with all dispatch. The enemy is receiving reinforcements daily and will no doubt increase to three or four thousand in four or five days. If this call is neglected, I am determined to sustain myself as long as possible and die like a soldier who never forgets what is due to his own honor and that of his country. VICTORY OR DEATH.

William Barret Travis
Lt. Col. Comdt.

Confident relief would arrive soon, the Texans victoriously defeated an attempt by the Mexicans on the third day to set up a battery only 300 yards south of the main Alamo gate. But that night, under the cover of darkness, the Mexicans succeeded, inching ever nearer the walls as more Mexican troops arrived.

Although the Mexicans kept up a steady cannonade, they bided their time for an all-out attack. The strategy was perhaps a result of Santa Anna's plan and his diversion. He looked on the Alamo as a trap and his underlings surmised he wanted to let more Texans in before he sealed them off. He fell in love with a beautiful young San Antonio *senorita*, Melchora Barrera, married her in a mock ceremony, and the Texans gained a little more time while he honeymooned.

With supplies and ammunition being hoarded against the big assault certain to come and tempers worsening inside the walls, Travis sent his best and perhaps only close friend inside the walls, Jim Bonham, out again to bring Fannin and his men back. Travis had sent couriers daily and no news came back. Travis told Bonham to offer Fannin joint command, anything to get him started. Bonham sneaked his horse down a tree-lined water ditch and escaped. Next day, Travis sent two more couriers to the colonies, imploring the settlers to hurry.

Davy Crockett was a blessing with his fiddle and his imaginative songs for the men who were cold and broken with fatigue from lack of sleep. He ridiculed Santa Anna, and it was funny until the men looked out over the walls and saw the Mexican army swollen every day with new arrivals.

While Crockett tried to keep up sagging spirits, a band of thirty-two men in Gonzales set out on February 29 for the Alamo, knowing they were on their way to certain death. Smith and Sutherland, dispatched by Travis on the first day, reached Gonzales on February 24 and found a little unit there waiting to march in with Fannin and other volunteers. By February 29, they knew Fannin was not going. So they set out with Smith. These were the bravest of the lot. They knew they weren't enough to matter. They knew that Sam Houston and other Texas leaders were on their way to the convention at Washington, 100 miles farther east of the Alamo than Gonzales. They couldn't abandon the men at the Alamo. And their deaths, if paid for dearly enough in time, might save their womenfolk and their town of Gonzales. This was the most they could hope for.

They slipped into the Alamo with no trouble from the Mexicans, but a Texan sentry shot one of them in the foot. Jubilation over the arrival of "Fannin and the Goliad boys!" ended abruptly when the besieged Texans realized there were just thirty-two volunteers from Gonzales. But the first disappointment over, the defenders recognized the courage of the men, who brought with them the flag that had defied the Mexicans on October 2 in the first battle of the revolution, and a celebration was held. More help *would* come.

But there was no need to wait for Fannin. That indecisive man made up his mind at last. He first set out for the Alamo February 28 with 400 men. A mile or so beyond his fort, three wagons broke down and that night at camp the oxen escaped. Fannin called a council. Should they proceed without artillery and with scant supplies? The vote was no. Fannin and his men re-crossed the river and went back to Fort Defiance. He had written off the Alamo; he had to prepare the next line of defense.

Alone, Jim Bonham rode back to the Alamo, his mission to Fannin again a failure. He charged through the opened south gate in a volley of enemy fire. Travis knew what the news would be. Only a Jim Bonham would have come back alone. Travis was grateful for that.

Now he had to tell the men that hope was over. He summoned them to the courtyard in front of the church, when there was a lull in the firing. The Mexicans followed their habit of siesta, the afternoon nap. Travis told the men he had sincerely believed help was on the way. Now it was clear he had been wrong. Fannin judged them lost beyond chance of rescue; Sam Houston was determined to set up first of all the authority of a legal Texas government to run the war.

No man, Travis told them, need feel any duty to stay any longer at the Alamo. There were still ways of escape, and escape had now become honorable. Couriers, about twenty of them, had made it through the Mexican lines. Bonham and Smith not only went out, but they also came back. The thirty-two men from Gonzales had got in unscathed two mornings ago. He was right. There was a "backdoor to the Alamo."

But he was going to stay he told them. Every man had the right of free choice. Dramatically, he pulled his sword from its sheath and drew a long line across the ground. "Let every man who will stay with me cross that line!" Young Tapley Holland leaped across, the first. All followed, except two men. One of these was a ghost-thin man on a cot. Jim Bowie, dying of pneumonia, asked for four men to lift his cot over the line. Cheers.

That left Moses Rose, a friend of Bowie, alone. He

was a soldier-of-fortune, having fought for Napoleon as a paid adventurer before coming to America. Soldiering was his trade. He fought to make money, not for ideals of freedom, liberty, or anything else. He no longer belonged with these dedicated men. He knew it, and they knew it too. They helped him over the wall when his bundle was ready, and he escaped disguised as a Mexican peon. He spoke Spanish like a native. He would escape.

So he did, and he lived to tell the tale. Rose's testimony is the only basis historians have for the matter of Travis' drawing the line, and some refuse to accept it. For most Texans, it is true. The line is drawn straight through their hearts, wrote J. Frank Dobie.

One other Texan left that night. John W. Smith, by now a perfect courier, took Travis' last letter to the Texas government in assembly at Washington-on-the-Brazos. Travis reviewed enemy activity from February 23 till March 3. (It was a Leap Year; February had 29 days.) He wrote: "We have been so fortunate as not to lose a man from any cause, and we have killed many of the enemy. The spirits of the men are still high though they have much to depress them. The determined valor and the desperate courage, heretofore exhibited by my men, will not fail them in the last struggle." He concludes as usual: "God and Texas—Victory or Death."

Smith carried with him all the letters the men could ready, along with keepsakes and mementoes for families. A calm acceptance of their sacrifice ruled the 182 men. Nineteen were from England and Europe, a scattering from the northern states, 32 from Tennessee, with other southern states represented by about a dozen each. There were nine or ten of Mexican descent, and they were the only ones who had been in Texas all their lives.

Smith also carried several personal letters of Travis, whose marriage back in Alabama had ended tragically. He had his six-year-old son in Texas—with friends at San Felipe. Hastily, on a piece of yellow wrapping paper that still survives, Travis wrote: "Take care of my little boy. If the country should be saved, I may make him a splendid fortune; but if the country should be lost . . . he will have nothing but the proud recollection that he is the son of a man who died for his country."

The men at the Alamo didn't know it, but they were now defending the independent Republic of Texas and not the Mexican Constitution of 1824, whose flag—perhaps along with others of various companies—waved above their mission-fortress. On March 2, the delegates to the convention had created a new Texas government, re-named Sam Houston commander-in-chief of its army, and at long last made a declaration of independence. Of this news, the men at the Alamo knew nothing, even though it was their resistance that made it possible.

Bitter, bleak weather blew in on the twelfth day of the siege, March 5. But Santa Anna silenced his guns for another reason. That afternoon he summoned his staff. The time had come. His instructions were precise though some of his generals wanted to delay the all-out assault till more cannon arrived from Saltillo. He stated a decisive blow must be struck. Tomorrow morning at four o'clock, under pre-dawn darkness but with sufficient light to scale the Alamo walls, the infantry would attack with ladders, charging from all four sides. The cavalry would back up the foot soldiers, to intercept escaping Americans—and to halt any Mexican retreat. Generalissimo Santa Anna would stand in readiness with the reserves. About 5,000 men would be grouped to storm the 182 Texans.

Craftily, Santa Anna allowed them to sleep, the sleep of exhaustion. It would take a while to come awake. His men would already be scaling the walls.

Travis wondered at the lull. Huddled against the freezing wind at their posts, the Texans slept. Three sentries stood guard outside; one man watched the fires within.

The Mexican army moved up its stations shortly after midnight, chilled to the marrow while waiting for the bugle call. When it came at last, they raced like mad to get warm, to get shelter from Texas guns.

The Texas sentries gave no alarm. Their throats must have been cut; a shot would have been warning to the men inside. The bugle blast brought the Texans awake, but its sound was as nothing compared to the drumming feet of the onrushing Mexican foot-soldiers. To this din, Santa Anna's regimental band added the famed Moorish battle march signifying no quarter, the *deguello*.

Travis raced to his station at the only part of the wall Mexican cannon had opened, a small breach on the north. He yelled to his men "to give 'em hell and do not surrender!" Davy Crockett and his Tennessee boys were on the south; Jim Bonham was directing the cannon on the east roof platform of the chapel; Jim Bowie, too near death to leave his cot, was surrounded with pistols and ready with his bowie knife.

The Mexican artillery slammed the fort with cannon balls. The Mexican infantry hoped to reach the shadow of the walls before the Texans could fire. The Texan cannon could not be maneuvered or fired downward from their fixed positions. But they caught the first Mexican advance before wall safety was reached. One Mexican corporal reported the slaughter was unbelievable. He counted forty corpses around him.

The generals ordered a retreat for re-grouping. The Texans caught their breath. They had a chance. Santa Anna couldn't afford losses like that. Same strategy on the next try. It wasn't long in coming. The Mexican generals didn't dare risk delay. Some of the units had lost half their men. The Mexican soldiers had shown high courage. But bravery has a time limit.

The second attack concentrated on Travis and the breach in the north wall. But the Texas guns picked off every Mexican who scaled a ladder to the top of the wall. As he tumbled below, he toppled over the ladder and the men on it. No ladder could stay up for long.

In the confusion, the Mexican troops sought union

and sought to escape the cannon firing in the four directions. The east units merged with those on the north and west. Again the losses were staggering. The bugles sounded retreat again.

The Mexican staff had learned a lesson. Travis' north wall offered the best chance of getting inside. For the third assault, which came with little delay, the Mexican columns—after feints at the other walls—massed opposite the breach. They were commanded to pour in. Again the *deguello*. Again the race for the walls. At enormous sacrifice, the dead trampled under foot, the living marching on top of their bodies, the Mexican infantry began to stream through the breach and on into the compound. Once inside, they knelt and started firing at the Texans on the wall platforms. In the half-light, the orange flare of gunpowder and the burst of cannon revealed position as much as did sight. Encounters were now at close range, bayonets and swords and bowie knives, even tomahawks, coming into play as guns emptied, or got too hot to handle, or were shot out of hand.

Travis may have been the first Texas casualty. He chose the most dangerous position. He was found dead with a pistol shot through his forehead. Some believe he committed suicide when he saw the north breach opened to a tide of invaders on the third attack. There is contrary evidence.

Once the Mexicans had a way in, sheer force of numbers meant the Texans no longer had a ghost of a chance. Knowing this, they meant to sell their lives at the highest price. If they knocked out a good chunk of this army, Santa Anna would have to put together another before he fought again.

On the west wall, some Texans managed to loosen their cannon and pivot it facing into the inside plaza. They got a deadly harvest before Mexican sharpshooters blasted them over the wall. The Mexicans then grabbed the cannon, worked it down the ramp to the ground and began blasting the next-to-last shelter of the Texans, the barracks building that formed the east wall of the plaza. Here the Texans had stacked defense parapets of cow hides enclosing a thick wall of dirt. But with the cannon now in Mexican possession, the doors were blasted in, men with bayonets charged through the openings and reduced the rooms one by one. Both sides fought like savages.

Davy Crockett and his men, defending the south stockade joining the chapel, died outdoors, with heaps of corpses around them. Davy lay in thick blood, his coonskin cap beside him, as a reliable account reported. The biggest pile of Mexican dead was found around Crockett's body.

The last refuge was the chapel, the only Alamo building that stands today. Here were the non-combatants in the Alamo, and the last remaining soldiers. Four or five Mexican women, wives or kin of the Mexicans who had chosen to fight alongside the Texans, were sheltered in the church, with their children. Here were Susanna Dickinson, wife of the Texas artillery expert, and her child in arms. Mrs. Dickinson was 18; the baby was 18 months. Bowie may have been here, or in the barracks. And here in the chapel was the powder storehouse of the Texans. They had agreed that the last man alive must put fire to it and blow up himself and all the Mexican army, it was hoped, with it.

The cannon blasted in the chapel door. The first Mexican soldiers to rush in were shot in the top of the head, from above. Only the cannon crews, on platforms up at the roof remained. The generals directed the fire upward. A brave and heroic Mexican on the Texan side, Gregorio Esparza, tumbled from the roof, caught by a bullet as he worked a gun with Jim Bonham. Esparza's wife and his four children were crouching in a corner below. He nearly fell straight into their arms. Bonham fell, then young Galba Fuqua, whose jaw had been shot off earlier and who tried pathetically to give some last message to Mrs. Dickinson. She couldn't make out a word.

Bowie was found and bayoneted over and over. He was known, and he was a great prize. His killers tossed him aloft on their bayonets like a bale of hay. And they saw Major Robert Evans, racing, torch in hand, toward the powder magazine. He was shot down on the run before he could hurl the fire for the blast.

The Texans had taken their last life. A few, seeking escape over the walls, were killed by the Mexican cavalry. Not a one of them was left. Or, did five men hide out, under mattresses, only to be found and shot? One Mexican officer so reported, claiming one of the men was Crockett. He added that these survivors pleaded for their lives. General Castrillon listened to their plea, but Santa Anna in a rage ordered their deaths. This is one of the many uncheckable accounts about the Alamo —accounts so filled with contradictions. Crockett, at least, was seen dead at his post by Mrs. Dickinson and others.

The exact number of Mexican dead is not known. Santa Anna's secretary, Ramon Caro, said: "We brought to San Antonio more than 5,000 men, and we lost during the siege 1,544 of the best of them. The Texans fought more like devils than men."

The fight took less than two hours on that Sunday morning, March 6, 1836. Santa Anna ordered a Christion burial for his dead. He had the Texans burned, piled in heaps, their bodies drenched in kerosene.

Sam Houston left Washington-on-the-Brazos for Gonzales on March 6, the day the Alamo fell. Travis' last news about the Alamo reached the convention March 6, four days after the delegates drafted the Texas Declaration of Independence. After praising his men, Travis doubts that Fannin will stir, and adds: "I hope your honorable body will hasten reinforcements. . . . Our supply of ammunition is limited."

As just re-named commander of the Texas army, Houston said, if time allowed, he would assemble volunteers who had reached Goliad or Gonzales, unite them with Fannin's 500 and save the Alamo. He sent a courier ahead to order Fannin to join him at Gonzales.

When news came through to Gonzales March 11 of the Alamo's fall, Houston faced a civilian population in panic. For the rest of the campaign, he was to have his burden of molding inexperienced volunteers into an army hampered by frightened settlers who dared not stay in their towns without defense and marched with the army. Gonzales was burned and abandoned to delay and impede the Mexican army.

Luckily, Santa Anna assumed the Alamo siege would kill off all resistance, and he rested on his laurels. He did not realize the Alamo battle would render Texas will invincible. He discovered his mistake six weeks later at the Battle of San Jacinto, April 21, 1836. In eighteen minutes of battle, Santa Anna's conquest of Texas evaporated in a staggering defeat. Texas independence was won—largely thanks to the legacy of needed time which the Alamo men bequeathed by their deaths.

The Texas Revolution decided, at last, who owned Texas, but it raised a question—Who owned the Alamo? The battles over the fortress-mission were not over. Much of its later history consists of litigation.

For the new Republic of Texas, there was no problem. The Alamo belonged to the Roman Catholic Church, by virtue of the transfer in 1794 of its records to the curacy of Bexar and the intended conversion of the Alamo Chapel into a parish church.

Nonetheless, by official "Acts of the Republic of Texas" on January 13 and 18, 1841, the "entire Alamo was granted" to Bishop John M. Odin as "Chief Pastor of the Roman Catholic Church in Texas" and to his successors in office.

But in 1851, the City of San Antonio instituted a suit in the District Court of Bexar County to recover this property, largely on the grounds that it was no longer being used for religious purposes. After Texas' annexation to the United States in 1846, the Bishop had leased the ruins to the U. S. government for use as a military quartermaster depot. Under Major Babbitt, some restoration had begun. The City of San Antonio, according to a deposition of Bishop Odin, was trying to sequester and seize the rental money for the buildings and church of the Alamo under, stated the Bishop, "some pretended claim." The trial and its appeal were both settled in favor of Bishop Odin.

In its summary of this case—"San Antonio vs. John Odin"—the Clerk's Office of the Supreme Court of Texas states that after the mission was secularized in 1794, the Indians remaining were sent to the missions of San Jose and Concepción, and that the friars continued to occupy the mission until 1801, when the soldiers of the "Flying Company" of Parras moved in. "The consent and permission of the Curate of the Parish was obtained at the time the troops took possession." (In fact, from then on the Alamo remained the chief military headquarters until 1836.) The summary also states that mass was said at the Alamo for the troops, and that such religious rites as baptisms, and marriages, and burials were performed for members of the soldiery.

It adds: "After the year 1835 these buildings were vacant, and in a very dilapidated condition, and so remained until 1841, when there were two or three families living in or occupying different rooms. They took possession without asking the consent of anyone. After being there two months, they were told by the Bishop at San Antonio that the property belonged to the church, and were requested to occupy and take care of the same for the church. The families remained there for ten months and then left."

When the Quartermaster of the United States Army took possession in 1847, he claimed the buildings belonged to the United States government, but a few months later acknowledged that he held them as tenant of the Bishop of Texas.

The City of San Antonio made its first claim to ownership of the mission remains in 1851, but based its right on the municipal act of incorporation of the city under the Republic of Texas laws in 1837, amended in another statute of 1838, and another of 1842. The city also claimed vague "former ownership."

But the court based its decision in favor of the Church primarily on the two acts of the Republic in 1841, which "granted and acknowledged" Catholic church ownership of the churches in San Antonio, Goliad, Victoria, and Nacogdoches, plus the churches at the missions of San Juan, Concepción, San Jose, Espada, the Alamo and the mission at Refugio. One interesting proviso, however, is that "nothing herein contained shall be so construed as to give title to any lands except the lots upon which the churches are situated which shall not exceed fifteen acres."

So the Bishop's lease to the United States army held. The army, making occasional improvements, used it until 1861—until the Confederates took over. After the end of the Civil War, the U. S. Army resumed possession and used it until 1876 when the quartermaster depot was transferred to the army's shining new Fort Sam Houston.

Then the Catholic Church decided to sell the property, for at least two reasons. In 1865 it had wanted to cancel its lease with the Army in order to convert the chapel into a church for "The German congregation." Happily for history and Alamo survival, no doubt, this plan failed when the Army firmly refused. There were no other adequate quarters available.

So, the Church of St. Joseph was built two blocks south of the Alamo, its inscriptions mingling Latin and German.

A second reason for the sale was the insistent commercial pressure of a growing community. Projects in the area abounded and the old mission was being put to curious uses. In the 1860's the south plaza wall, housing the Spanish soldiers' guardhouse, had become a police station.

Commercial interests were anxious to have the land in the heart of the city that soon became the largest and dominant metropolis in the state. And the State of

Texas, old enough to treasure now its past, wanted to acquire the Alamo.

First purchaser was a French business wizard, Honore Grenet who purchased "all the interest of the Roman Catholic Church in the Alamo Property" from Bishop A. D. Pellicer on November 30, 1877 for $20,000. Specifically exempt from this sale, however, was the chapel itself, plus certain land the State of Texas contemplated buying from the Church.

This contemplated state purchase became fact under an official act of April 23, 1883. The State of Texas placed the Alamo Chapel, which Governor Ireland bought from the Church for $20,000, under the custody of the City of San Antonio, which agreed to care for the building and allocate a salary for a custodian. Fortunately, in 1871, the corporate city of San Antonio had bought from Bishop Dubuis the Catholic property extending westward from Alamo Plaza to the river, agreeing to dedicate this area to public use as an open space and to be joined with the Alamo Plaza and the Plaza de Valero above and below the purchased tract forming one central and public Alamo Plaza.

The agreement between the State of Texas and the City of San Antonio prevailed until 1905, but there was one terrible flaw in the Alamo's new status as a public monument. Honore Grenet's heirs sold his commercially exploited part of the Alamo property—which included the Monastery House or later "barracks"—to the firm of Hugo and Schmeltzer in 1886. This meant that the Alamo Chapel was adjoined by a thriving wholesale enterprise and what some ladies of the town called a "Whisky House."

Grenet, in a burst of patriotism *a la francaise*, had designed his Alamo Store to harmonize with the Chapel, or so he thought. Remodeling the old convent he added two wooden towers and emplaced wooden cannon along them. To the satisfaction of most residents, these martial decorations could not survive an ill wind, or storm, that blew somebody good.

Sentiment, meantime, was growing in the state for preserving the Alamo properly as a memorial. By 1905, the state legislature empowered the Governor to buy up the business property adjoining the Alamo Chapel.

But a far-sighted and spirited officer of the Daughters of the Republic of Texas had already beat the state to this patriotic deed. She was Clara Driscoll (Mrs. Hal Sevier), also an officer of the Texas Federation of Women's Clubs.

The Daughters of the Republic of Texas were organized in 1891 and were fervently energetic in preserving historical relics. Fearful of commercial attempts to exploit the Alamo property, Clara Driscoll worked with the DRT chapters, raising about $7,000, and bought the Hugo-Schmeltzer property, saving it for the state. She posted the cash in hand of the Daughters' fund plus about $18,000 of her own to make the $25,000 down payment and signed notes for the remaining $50,000 required.

When the State Legislature, under Governor S. W. T. Lanham, allocated $65,000 for the purchase, Clara Driscoll and the Daughters of the Republic of Texas sold it back to the state. Their purchase agreement had expressly stated: "It is distinctly understood and agreed that this property is purchased by Clara Driscoll for the use and benefit of the Daughters of the Republic of Texas, and is to be used by them for the purpose of making a park about the Alamo, and for no other purpose whatever."

So, the State of Texas assigned custody of these re-assembled portions of the Alamo compound to the Daughters of the Republic of Texas. In their patriotism, they accepted this custody, assuming all responsibility for providing funds for maintenance and upkeep. What they have done is a priceless and selfless service to the state.

Nonetheless, by 1909, The Daughters of the Republic of Texas, meeting in annual session April 20-22 at San Antonio, passed a resolution asking the State to take charge of the custody and specifically that "a commission of not less than five persons, to be male citizens of the State of Texas" be appointed by the Governor to assume the custody and care of the Alamo.

What had happened? The resolution states that conditions have arisen which "make it expedient" to take this action. The conditions are vaguely stated; in the defense of their trust and custody, the Daughters "have been forced into the courts, and have had to resort to contentious measures altogether distasteful, and unbecoming to the dignity of this great organization."

In essence, there was a division within the group over what to do about the Hugo & Schmeltzer building. The great majority of the chapters held to the view that Honore Grenet's "restoration" was raised on walls fronting the old Convent and that only these walls should be left standing. But the Adina de Zavala Chapter of San Antonio—headed by the granddaughter of the famous Mexican member of Santa Anna's cabinet who had bravely joined the Texans in their revolution— maintained that the commercial structure was built on the foundations of the Convent itself and; therefore, it should be restored rather than demolished.

The evidence was contradictory. When Santa Anna set out in 1836 from the Alamo to pursue Sam Houston's army, he left General Andrade in charge at the Alamo with 400 men. He left orders to clean up the fort and make it functional in case the Texans were able to organize a renewed battle for its possession or a sneak attack. These orders were countermanded after the defeat at San Jacinto; the Alamo was now to be demolished. It is not known to what extent Andrade followed this order. One Mexican soldier described the smoke billowing as the troops pulled out. Did Andrade try to demolish the battered Convent or "barracks"? San Antonio citizens with long memories, or family memoirs, were called to testify about the condition of the Alamo after the Mexican evacuation. Their testimony was vastly contradictory, an affliction that has made much

Alamo history, of necessity, a matter of intelligent surmise.

The complicated quarrel is made somewhat clear by the harrassment of Governor O. B. Colquitt in a "peace conference" he called for "those interested in the Alamo" at the Saint Anthony Hotel in San Antonio, December 28, 1911.

Governor Colquitt had three reasons for calling a peace conference: (1) he was at odds with the Daughters over how to restore the property and what to make of it; (2) the Adina de Zavala chapter, or at least Miss de Zavala and twelve members loyal to her, steadily kept up litigation to secure control of the Alamo to her San Antonio chapter; (3) this internal squabble meant that the Alamo was being badly kept. Whatever the legitimate aims of Miss Adina de Zavala, her methods were disturbingly litigious.

At last, in 1910, the Texas Supreme Court settled the internal dispute within the Daughters of the Republic by a decision which said the group led by Miss Driscoll was the legal Daughters of the Republic organization.

But Miss De Zavala didn't stop her fight.

The Governor made it plain in advance that he was going to assume full authority. The meeting would pointedly refuse to hear any dispute between the chapters of the Daughters. He himself thought that both the Chapel and the Hugo & Schmeltzer building were parts of the Alamo defended by the Texans, but at any event, he wanted to restore the Alamo to the state it was in when the siege took place. He didn't plan to restore a Franciscan mission. He was not going back beyond 1836. What he wanted was a preservation of the Alamo as it was in its most historic moment.

This was a limited—and short-sighted—viewpoint, but even in this he was inevitably somewhat disappointed. After hearing hours of testimony and pleading for accurate information, he said somewhat bitterly: "Now, I think we all understand each other, and I have gained about as much information as I had when I came. If there is anybody who knows more about the Alamo than I do, come up here and let us have the information. Now I want you to go with me to the Alamo. I am going to point out what I intend to tear down. You might talk to me a thousand years and you couldn't change my opinion about tearing those parts down."

At the inspection, one faction still maintained that the wooden superstructure continued two-storey high stone walls that were part of the monastery; the other faction claimed the building's stone walls were only eight feet high, constituting a sort of "fence" for the monastery located farther back and now disappeared.

The Bishop of San Antonio promised the Governor he would send a translation of all the church's records pertaining to the Alamo to Austin.

It was a peace conference of a sort. The Governor had really opposed every faction. He wasn't going to reconstitute the mission. He didn't want a "monument" added to the grounds. As he said, "Texas could build a monument 7,000 feet high, and it wouldn't commemorate their deeds like these buildings." Nor was he interested in a park. "We can cultivate flowers elsewhere."

But at least one thing was clear. Texans did care about the Alamo—enough to fight over it—and did intend to preserve it for posterity. The Alamo battle, or battles, was of consuming public interest.

Peace was restored. Newspaper coverage of the problems aroused interest and the Daughters began to get cooperation from many sources. The Hugo & Schmeltzer building was torn down, but its west (Convent) wall properly remained standing. Other unsightly sheds and structures around the chapel were removed.

Allocation of Texas Centennial Celebration Funds in 1936 from the City of San Antonio and the State of Texas made possible the Alamo park with the whole enclosure now containing seven or eight acres. The Alamo Museum was built just north of the chapel, removing display cases from the chapel and allowing it the sense of space and quiet a chapel should have. The Alamo library and its adjoining meeting hall were added. A great service to scholars and students, the library also houses the fascinating early paintings made by the young French settler at Castroville, Theodore Gentilz.

In addition, the Daughters have twice repaired the roof over the chapel which was erected by the U. S. Quartermaster Corps in 1848, when the side and back walls were also raised and the unauthentic parapet added to cap the front wall.

Despite the ravages of time and battle, the Alamo retains its mood and its spell. All who enter there feel it at once.

And so the mission that had survived a uniquely versatile career as: religious center, fort, hospital, prison, military warehouse, hostel, police station, housing unit, mercantile enterprise, birthplace of two "Republics of Texas," contested in ownership by Roman Catholic Church, City of San Antonio, Confederacy, State of Texas, and the United States Government—at last became what it was originally meant to be: a shrine for civilized, enlightened, and purposeful man.

Not beautiful like San Jose, nor Mission Concepción, lacking the nostalgic charm of Capistrano and San Francisco de la Espada, it is nonetheless the most haunting of all the San Antonio missions.

And yet, its facade, the unrestored authentic lower part, is a lovely and delicate miracle of survival. Its rounded arched portal, six feet wide and about twelve feet high, with its keystone of flat, continuous carving suggests in its rich detail the Moorish influence on Spain, its carved leaves and arabesques making the stone quiver with the play of shadows and light. And the flanking columns on either side of the doorway, deepening the niches for the statues of saints (appropriately for the imagination, blank), delight the eye with their halfway fluting, soaring upward, which ends in twisted spirals, crowned by nests of leaves. Foliage forms are everywhere, symbolizing renewal.

The last word may be left to J. Frank Dobie, who speaks for all of us when he writes:

"When I was seventeen years old, my mother and father brought my older sister and me to San Antonio for the annual fair. This was in the fall of 1905. I think we rode in an automobile. I remember some of the sights at the fair grounds. I remember the impression of city streets, but far above all I remember the Alamo. That first visit has never faded. . . .

"There weren't many other people in the old building. It was silent and the light was dim. All the small rooms and some of the spots in the big room, which had been the chapel, bore markers saying that here Bowie died, here the 'Babe of the Alamo' and her mother had slept, and so on. My imagination was so fired that I was in a kind of fever. . . .

"I cannot remember when the word Alamo was not familiar, connoting drama, heroic action, nobility."

And this connotation, one might add, includes the Franciscan friars as well as the Texas fighters for independence.

La Bahia

La Bahia

La Bahia

by
Joe B. Frantz

The threads reach as far back as the historian, the anthropologist, and the archeologist can stretch the time of man upon this earth. Early man moved down this continent of North America, working his way around the green glacial lakes, through hairbreadth defiles and *canons* cut by streams determined to escape beyond the mountain barriers, and onto the corky, flat floor of the Southwestern plains and deserts. He was seeking what man has always sought—something to eat, somewhere to live, a way to keep warm—a way to live.

At various places along the trail some men thought they had found their way of life, and dropped out. Others, though, pushed on, until they left behind the easier game, the richer berries and fruits, and found themselves trapped in a region poor in yield and destined to be poor in culture.

Centuries later when Cabeza de Vaca saw these people along the Texas Gulf Coast, he observed that they were "great in hunger, thirst, and cold, as if they were made for the endurance of these more than other men, by habit and nature." By now they were known as Karankawas—or, if you walked far enough inland, Coahuiltecans. Like any great group, they were divided into smaller tribes, each with its own name and its differing characteristics. But wherever they were, and whatever their names, they constituted a dismal lot, undefeated by their environment but not exactly triumphant either.

The tribes that roamed the area around the later San Antonio and Guadalupe river valleys were mainly Aranamas and Tamiques. A dozen bands or so, they brought little history with them, and have left little impact on Texas culture. They had chosen the Brush Country, a featureless land of scrub and shrub and generally hostile to being lived off. But there they had lived, had survived, for thousands of years — on the *tuna* of the cactus plant, on sotol, on pecans, and on mesquite beans. Once in awhile game varied the diet—an occasional wandering bison, rodents, reptiles, and bugs; or the game which is still hunted today—the deer and the javelina.

These Indians developed no agriculture. Even today, with all the devices of the mid-twentieth century the white man farms only when some irrigation project makes it possible. Mainly today's inhabitant raises cattle, though some try corn, cotton, grain sorghum, and grass seed. The lush fields of garden truck lie elsewhere in Texas; the largest city in 1960 was Goliad, with 1,782 persons. Exploding population, urban sprawl— these are not problems for this area.

So the crude people entered the region, and remained crude and static. They learned to survive in the prehistoric past, and they never changed the pattern. Few invaders bothered them, for no one else wanted the region. As W. W. Newcomb has pointed out, from the anthropologist's viewpoint, "south Texas has the appearance of a relict region, an isolated backwash in which cultures remained virtually unchanged for long periods."

When Cabeza de Vaca found them—or perhaps more precisely, when they found him—he saw nearly naked men in breechclouts, fiber sandals, and now and then a robe, dedicated or doomed to a life of wandering in search of subsistence. They ate well when the brush was greening or the nuts were falling, and they fought starvation with the onset of each dreary winter. When they hunted, they hunted communally, with stakes, pitfalls, brush fires, and bows and arrows. When they ate, they ate everything—meat and fish, naturally, but also larvae, spiders, ant eggs, earth, and deer dung.

They knew mescal, and they knew peyote, that hallucinating tea recently "discovered" by the twentieth century beatnik. Since they could weave and tan, they lived in huts of reed mats and hides, easily put up and as easily taken down for the time of moving on. They were not above eating a captive Indian taken in one of their sporadic fights. They liked to tattoo themselves.

Other Spaniards after de Vaca wandered or blundered through the area inhabited by these wilderness children, but none chose to remain. From an Indian standpoint life remained free.

But nearly two centuries later a foreign strand is introduced into the fabric with the coming of a French nobleman, Robert Cavalaier, Sieur de La Salle, the man who had claimed the interior of the North American continent for his glorious Louis XIV. On August 1, 1684, La Salle had left France with about three hundred countrymen aboard four ships to found an empire at the mouth of the Mississippi River. Whether he intended to overshoot or whether he was confused by Gulf of Mexico currents, which even today cause United States and Mexican shrimpers to go astray, the fact remains that he missed the mouth of his Father of Waters, landing instead at Matagorda Bay in Texas. Near the mouth of Garcitas Creek he erected Fort St. Louis, and set out soon to explore the land about him. Gone was his *St. Francois*, lost to Spanish corsairs; his *Amiable* and *Belle* had wrecked on the Texas shores; and his fourth ship, the *Joli*, had belied its name by unhappily deserting him for an immediate return to France. The beginning foretold the end. Things were bad, but they could be worse; and shortly they were. Somehow La Salle survived for more than two years, when one of his men decided both he and the leader would be better off with La Salle in an afterworld.

Fort St. Louis was a failure, if one looks for permanence. But it accomplished a greater purpose, for its short life convinced the Spaniards that the neglected Texas *llano* deserved Spanish attention. Texas might be an inhospitable land, insofar as nearly two hundred years of Spaniards in the New World were concerned; but if the French coveted it, Texas must be secured for Spain.

The result was an expedition from Monclova under Governor Alonso de León, the first to visit the future site of La Bahía presidio and mission. The date was April 22, 1689, nearly two hundred years after Columbus had sailed to the New World and 147 years, lacking one day, till Texas would win her right to stand alone in the world. De León found two Frenchmen living with the Indians, not much of a French heritage but enough to spark a Spanish impulse.

Even then, events moved slowly around the Fort St. Louis region. Another one-third of a century was to pass—thirty-three years of considerable Spanish mission activity in Texas—before a wealthy Coahuilan, the Marqués de San Miguel de Aguayo, governor and captain-general of the province of the Tejas and New Philippines, would set out with 500 men, plus horses, cattle, and sheep, to shore up the sagging Spanish mission system and to found new presidios and missions where security and Christianity could march together. In the spring of 1722 Aguayo directed construction of both presidio and mission at La Bahía del Espíritu Santo, or Lavaca Bay, near the site of La Salle's old fort, leaving ninety soldiers to defend against danger. Here would be a good place to domesticate and Christianize the savage Indian; here, too, would be a good place to guard against incursions from the sea, whether they be by the exploratory descendants of La Salle or the bumptious, burgeoning English whose greed carried them all too regularly into regions the Spanish felt belonged to them.

La Bahía then became an actuality. It was not one of the truly early missions, and from a teaching standpoint it was not one of the great religious centers. It was not even located on its final site. But as a recurring scene of spilled blood, wrecked ambitions, grandiose schemes, and dramatic conflict, La Bahía stands alone. It cannot compete with the Alamo as a shrine of testimony to all that early Texans strived for and to the freedom that men throughout the world and throughout time have hungered for, but for repetitive, continuing tragedy, La Bahía is the Texan home for Melpomene. No buskined Athenian could have created a more congenially menacing stage for the muse of tragedy than those Franciscan fathers from Zacatecas who chose La Bahía to introduce the sunshine of this world and the next to the undesiring aborigine.

Accordingly, let us skip the detailed development of La Bahía and move almost directly to the black practice of its bloody dramaturgy. En route it should suffice to say that the Indians were instructed and domesticated with the usual intermittent success and heartbreak attending the efforts of the *padres* at the other Texas missions described in this book. Some captains of the presidio proved honest, while some were corrupt. Consequently, sometimes the soldiers were paid and disciplined, and sometimes they were as nearly naked as the Aranamas and would have been as happy to run away if they had known anywhere to escape to. Now and again the Comanches and the Lipan Apaches intruded, and now and again they were run off after some depredations. Some souls were saved, while others were merely interrupted. The number of livestock, especially cattle, increased, which would be important after the American Civil War, because this area would lie alongside the seed ground of the range cattle industry in the United States.

Twice the presidio and mission were moved. In the fall of 1723 a quarrel between the soldiers and the Indians led to flight and reprisal, a pastime that continued for a quarter of a century. Father Peña, one of the original missionaries, had written that the tribes around La Bahía "were very docile and would enter readily upon the work of cultivating the earth and their own souls, the more because they live in greater misery than the other tribes, since they subsist altogether upon fish and go entirely without clothing." But as one historian observed sixty years ago, Father Peña "proved himself either ignorant or defiant of history, a bad sociologist, and a worse prophet."

The result was that the leaders, both clerical and secular, decided that some other area might be more fertile, both physically and spiritually. Just four years after their founding, both presidio and mission were removed inland to the bank of the Guadalupe River near the present city of Victoria. Although La Bahía has been a memory for more than two centuries, people around Victoria still identify the region as Mission Valley.

Again, the location failed to satisfy, and in 1749 the mission-fort was moved to its "permanent" site on the banks of the San Antonio River, where its real history was to begin—and to terminate. Four years later another mission was added nearby, when the mission, Nuestra Señora del Rosario, about two leagues from La Bahía, was added to the guardianship of the presidio.

When Fray Gaspar José de Solís visited the missions in 1767-1768, he noted that the mission Indians were "given to idleness and arrogance," and were "cowards and pusilanimous," a word that Theodore Roosevelt would resurrect later to describe the neutrality of Woodrow Wilson. When he arrived at La Bahía, forty "Indians on horseback, armed with guns, came out in two lines making a skirmish to receive me." He found, as it still can be found, the mission on one side of the San Antonio, and the royal presidio on the other bank. Communication was by canoe.

"The ornaments, sacred vessels and all things that pertain to Divine worship are very clean, very neat and in due arrangement," the *padre* wrote. "All the Indians of this mission guarded the Holy Sacrament by day and by night, acting guard continually at the door of the chapel. They burned the lamp with nut oil. . . ."

The mission called for two priests paid by the King "(may he rest in glory)," but only one was serving the faithful at the time of de Solís' visit. This Franciscan,

Father Francisco López, had managed to accumulate considerable property. Under his benign guidance were eight herds of animals, including "four droves of burros" which "produce many mules," plus one hundred "gentle horses, about seventy gentle mules, . . . fifteen hundred head of sheep and goats, two hundred yoke of oxen, big fields for planting corn. Everything depends on the rain because they do not have water nor can it be taken from the river or from any other place." (Author's note: this sounds more contemporary than spiritual and historical.) About the only jarring discord was the Indian preference of "diabolical *mitotes*," all-night feasts and dances with a firm base of peyote, eaten green or dried, or drunk as a tea. No two *mitotes* followed the same procedure, but in general, according to Newcomb, the evening went something like this:

"The guests, attired in their best finery, assembled sometime before dark. Soon after dark a large fire was started, meat was put on to roast, and music for dancing commenced. A drum, made by stretching a coyotehide over a wooden hoop, and a gourd rattle were used to accompany the singing onlookers. The dancers, both men and women, soon began to circle the fire in time to the pulsating music. They danced with their bodies close together, their shoulders moving slightly, their feet close together, from which position they progressed by a series of hops, all in time with the music. The dancing went on the entire night without pause. Peyote was passed at intervals, and occasionally some of the dancers fell into trances. Among some groups, those who had fallen into this peyote stupor were roused by being scratched with a sharp-toothed instrument until the blood flowed freely. . . . This ceremonial dance and the festivities were ended by daybreak, the guests departing with any remaining food."

This was religion? Not to a Christian priest, who could see only the pagan aspects. But the dancing expressed the soul of the Indian, and the peyote brought him face to face with his Christian God or with the gods of his fathers. And the priest, who preached simple worship and the beauty of orderly, every-day routine, just could not erase the devotions of generations. He could only complain, as did Father de Solís, of "their natural inconstancy" and praise the local priests for sponsoring dances "accompanied by the music of the violin and guitar" which might lead to more temperate nights and less temptation to "go off to the woods and dance." Faith, perseverance, and patience in equal quantities were necessary to sustain a priest at La Bahía.

Gradually La Bahía went downhill, both physically and in its spiritual drive. However, when other missions in Texas were being secularized and their properties divided among the Christian adherents, the La Bahía complex continued. The Indians simply refused, in the opinion of the Spanish, to become responsible, so that it was impossible to turn over any property to them. The presidio remained necessary, both because of alarums from the coast and because of threats from Comanche and Apache. Periodically some Indian was always seeing a French crew or a British landing, so that the military could never entirely relax. Although most of the dangers proved to be as visionary as a peyote dream, to take a chance might prove fatal. So the fort and the missions continued into the nineteenth century, poverty-stricken and always on the edge of dissolution but somehow holding together. Meanwhile a third mission, Nuestra Señora del Refugio, "one of the last flickers of ebbing Spanish energy," had been assigned to the care of the presidio in 1793. Now all three missions and the fort could starve together.

No better example of the futility of life at La Bahía can be found than in the construction of its irrigation dam. The dam had been authorized—nay, demanded—when the mission had been established at mid-century. Precious time that might have been better spent in planting crops or herding livestock, or even saving souls, had gone into construction of this dam. When later a captain had told the Spanish governor that erection of the dam was impossible, he had been ordered to put his men back to work on it. When La Bahía was finally abandoned more than three-quarters of a century after its location along the San Antonio, the dam was still unconstructed, but it was worked on till the very last. Meanwhile the garrison flirted with starvation for want of irrigation of its crops.

In fact, as late as 1825, only five years before the missions were secularized, Alcalde Juan José Hernandez wrote his political chief that to turn over mission lands to the Aranamas and Acomas in the area would cause their reversion to primitivism. One hundred years of work had left the Indian wards still "shiftless and lazy" and beyond "hope of becoming useful to the nation unless they are subjected rigorously to law and punishment."

As for protection, the forces of La Bahía were impotent at best. In the spring of 1822, for instance, the Comanches had raided the town, stolen the horses of the presidio's cavalry, and carried off five prisoners. On another occasion one reporter doubted that the garrison could raise six mounted men to pursue any sort of enemy. The pacified Indians, it appears, only lived near the missions when the seasons were unfavorable—or, in other words, when it suited them.

But already what activity this mission had seen. True, it had been written off in 1822 as beyond rehabilitation, its church destroyed, its walls in ruins, its bells silent, and only fifteen of its Indians available for work. Nonetheless it was a place of importance, a place to take, a place to head for.

For instance, there had been the Gutiérrez-Magee expedition, known to Texans and Mexicans with equal admiration and regret. José Bernardo Gutiérrez de Lara had tried unsuccessfully to dislodge the Spanish from North Mexico. At 37 years of age, still trying, he had come to Louisiana to raise money and followers for further revolution. There he met Augustus William

Magee, a native of Boston, third in his West Point graduating class, and just passed over for promotion by Washington politics. Gutiérrez and Lieutenant Magee set out to free Texas and as much beyond as possible. Around Nacogdoches in the summer of 1812 they were successful, and so they pressed on. By November they had reached La Bahía, where Magee, though in command, was fighting a harder battle with either malaria or consumption than with the Spanish.

On the approach of the Republicans the Spanish guardians of the presidio fled. On November 13, 1812, the Royalists returned to lay siege. They tried an assault, but were repulsed. They then dug in for four months, with the monotony broken only by an occasional skirmish in which the Republicans at least maintained the miserable *status quo*. The most noted of the engagements took place in late January, 1813, the so-called battle of the White Cow. One of the sides was trying to capture a white cow to beef up its diet— (sources are divided as to which side was chasing the poor creature)—when the other side became covetous. The Republicans reputedly lost one killed and six wounded, the Spaniards more heavily. History is silent on whether the cow was a casualty also.

Two weeks later the two contestants fought from daybreak until late afternoon. This time the Spaniards drove the Republicans out of the fort, only to be driven out in turn. Three times that day the Spaniards drove in, and three times they backed right out again.

About this time Magee died—of consumption, by suicide, by poison—take your choice of reporters. Of him, Gutiérrez had said that he "was a man of military genius, but very cowardly." Gutiérrez may not have been entirely fair to his partner, for certainly Magee had shown courage in the past. And certainly the facts show that Magee held out against a superior force that may often have outnumbered him. Succeeding Magee as commander within the fort was a Virginian named Samuel Kemper, who lifted the siege, pursued the flee-

ing Royalists to San Antonio, and there whipped them
again. La Bahía had its Alamo experience, but with a
more pleasant ending.

Four years later La Bahía re-enters the historical
arena. Henry Perry, a Connecticut soldier of fortune
who had survived the Gutiérrez-Magee expedition, joined Francisco Xavier Mina for an invasion of Mexico in
the spring of 1817. Dissatisfied, Perry left Mina with
about fifty men to invade Texas. On June 17 he demanded the surrender of La Bahía, but his timing was
unfortunate. A royal force under Governor Antonio
María Martínez, already underway, showed up that
same afternoon. Perry did not wait for the enemy but
fled at once for Nacogdoches. Caught up with, all but
four of Perry's force were killed or wounded. Perry
himself committed suicide to avoid capture. Once again,
La Bahía had tasted blood.

Texas would not stay quiet, and La Bahía was caught
up in the continual cross-fire. James Long, a twentyish
former Virginian better known for his wife, Jane, was
one of the many Mississippians who looked on the Ad-
ams-Oñis Treaty as an American surrender. About
$500,000 was subscribed to correct partially the newly-
established boundaries of the Louisiana Purchase by
dissecting Texas from Spain. Long made the first run
on Texas in 1819, but when an alliance with the pirate,
Jean Laffite, and promised aid from Natchez did not
materialize, the Long expedition had to flee back to the
safety of Natchitoches and New Orleans. In 1820 Dr.
Long returned to the Galveston Bay area, worked on
plans with such men as José Bernardo Gutiérrez de Lara
(still hopeful), José Felix Trespalacios, and Ben Milam,
and on September 19, 1821, set out with fifty-two men
to capture La Bahía.

Taking La Bahía proved no problem. Holding the
fort did. Four days after Long had taken the presidio,
Spanish forces under former Governor Ignacio Pérez,
who had chased Long out of Texas the first time, moved
into La Bahía, quickly subdued its captors, and returned

to San Antonio with Long as their prisoner. With the coming of Mexican independence Long was released from prison and given permission to go to Mexico City to obtain full pardon or even tangible gratitude from President Iturbide.

Iturbide, however, was uncertain about the intensity of Long's great revolutionary flame. "I want to know," he wrote to Colonel Trespalacios, who had obtained Long's release, "the true character of the Long expedition and why they seized La Bahía after it had already proclaimed independence. They seem no less than invaders in spite of all their protests. . . . Nevertheless all efforts will be made to determine the truth." What the general truth was will probably never be known, but one specific truth is. On May 8, 1822, Long was shot by a Mexican guard for refusing to halt when challenged. Rumor was that his death had been ordered by Colonel Trespalacios, now governor of the imperial province of Texas. Wife Jane Long, of course, lived on for nearly sixty years more as Texas' most famous widow, its first boardinghouse keeper, and its so-called Mother of Texas.

As tension heightened between Mexico and her Texas province, it was only natural that the settlement around La Bahía should be involved. In 1829 the state congress for Coahuila y Texas had declared that the presidio of La Bahía was henceforth the town of Goliad, a name generally considered an anagram of the name of the patriot Hidalgo, with the Spanish "H" silent. The town looked like any sun-baked Mexican town, with its better homes one-storied, flat-roofed, and of stone, while its poor huddled in miserable *jacales* of sticks, straw, and mud, not much better than the portable Indian huts of a century before.

When in September, 1835, Santa Anna's brother-in-law, General Martín Perfecto de Cós, learned that the Mexican revenue vessel, *Correo Mexicano*, had been captured by Texans, he set out from Matamoros to reinforce Goliad and Bexar. On October 2 General Cós occupied Goliad, and then with more than four hundred men pressed inland, leaving only the normal complement of thirty *presidiales* to guard the place. On the night of October 9 a Texan force under Captain George M. Collinsworth marched into the fort, beat down its doors, and after a short fight took the town in the name of Texas. General Cós was cut off from his supply line to the Gulf of Mexico, a situation that would hamper the Mexican effort until the following spring.

On the following December 20 the group in charge at Goliad anticipated the Texas leaders by two and one-half months by drawing up and signing a Goliad Declaration of Independence. Ninety-one men, including two of Mexican descent, signed the document, which pledged the signers to dedicate their lives, fortunes, and honor to obtaining and sustaining the "free, sovereign, and independent State" of Texas. The *ad interim* Texas government in San Felipe was annoyed and embarrassed by what it considered a premature document, especially since the General Council was hoping it could obtain assistance from the federalists in northern Mexico. Accordingly, the declaration was "buried," and the Goliad declaration has been little celebrated. Premature or not, it showed the spirit which motivated the community.

The bloodiest event for which La Bahía and Goliad are remembered is, of course, the Goliad Massacre. Its details are so well-known as to be superfluous here. In its broad outlines the story tells how Colonel James W. Fannin, a West Point-trained agitator for a Texas revolution, landed at Copano at the beginning of February, 1836; joined his two hundred men with others at Refugio, San Patricio, and elsewhere; and established headquarters at Goliad. There Fannin put his men to work rebuilding the old presidio, meanwhile keeping in touch with independent operations aimed beyond the Rio Grande and with William B. Travis's forces at the Alamo.

At one time Fannin considered moving his headquarters to Bexar. On February 25 he received a call for help from Travis. Fannin decided to go to the Alamo's relief, but when a wagon broke down two miles from La Bahía, he decided he had gone far enough. Military tacticians agree that at this juncture Colonel Fannin should have abandoned Goliad, sparing his men to fight the forces of General Santa Anna under more favorable terms. Instead, he continued fortifying the presidio, which he had now named Fort Defiance.

When General Sam Houston learned of the fall of the Alamo, he sent a messenger to Colonel Fannin, directing him to withdraw his forces to Victoria as soon as possible. Still Fannin delayed. When in mid-March Fannin's situation had become desperate, he prepared to move. But mainly he "prepared" instead of moving, loading too much artillery, awaiting a favorable night, and counseling with his officers. Despite the disastrous time spent getting ready, the troops left without their rations, which had been burned. Hungry oxen, necessary for moving artillery and baggage, had been starving in the corrals. Once on the trail their hunger took command, and they went where they pleased in search of grass. They could not be directed. Even then, Fannin might have made his escape if he had not decided to rest his men on the broad prairie instead of nearby Coleto woods.

Here the Mexicans under General Urrea surrounded the waterless, foodless Texans—three hundred inexperienced troops against a thousand battle-hardened Mexicans. The Texans gave a good account of themselves and again might have escaped if they had not insisted on remaining behind to tend their wounded. From a devotion standpoint their attitude represents true humanity; from a military standpoint, this attitude spelled sheer suicide.

Two hundred thirty four Texans were marched back to Goliad, assured that they would be treated as prisoners of war. The next day fifty wounded joined them. On March 25 about eighty more men from William

Ward's Georgia Battalion were herded in. All looked forward to being released to the United States soon. When General Santa Anna learned of General Urrea's promised clemency, he ordered immediate execution of the "perfidious foreigners."

On the morning of March 27, 1836, three divisions of Texas prisoners were marched down three roads leading away from La Bahía. Still within earshot of the place where the Franciscan fathers had tried to teach gentleness and an end to savagery, shots rang out at almost point-blank range. Those surviving were chased like game, and either shot or bayoneted. Within the fort Fannin and forty wounded were killed. Altogether 342 men were executed that day; only 28 escaped, plus 20 more who were useful as doctors, nurses, or mechanics. In the history of infamy Goliad had now taken its place.

As every follower of the Texas story knows, these deaths were unnecessary, for less than four weeks later the Texans under General Houston had routed the Mexicans at San Jacinto, and Texas was free to make her own way in the world.

It was the end of La Bahía and its missions in the public eye. Nuestra Señora del Espíritu Santo de Zuñiga, Nuestra Señora del Refugio, and Nuestra Señora del Rosario had joined the historic story of man's spiritual search for a better world; while the presidio, Nuestra Señora de Loreto, and its chapel have remained as a visible shrine where brave men dared and where men of all sorts—brave, cowardly, treacherous, impetuous, timid, savage, and unflinching—lived and died in the effort to transform a nearly barren land into a land where families could some day follow without fear the mandate of the American Declaration of Independence guaranteeing to every man "life, liberty, and the pursuit of happiness."

Mission Concepcion

Mission Concepcion

Concepcion

by

Joseph W. Schmitz, S.M.

The five Spanish missions located in and about San Antonio are justly famous and attract a great number of tourists annually. Undoubtedly the Alamo—Mission San Antonio de Valero—known as the cradle of Texas liberty, is the most renowned of all. For architectural splendor Mission San José is unsurpassed and generally recognized as the "queen of the missions." San Juan Capistrano and San Francisco de la Espada are likewise impressive reminders of bygone days. Mission Purísima Concepción, sometimes known as the best preserved of the missions, has a fame of its own and an interesting history which merits exploration.

Missions were religious institutions erected by the Spaniards, usually on a frontier, to hold and extend control of their lands. They were agencies of the Church and of the State, established to Christianize and civilize the Indian. The Spanish clergy who labored in the missions, while primarily interested in Christianizing the Indians, knew full well that unless and until the Indian learned and absorbed the rudiments of civilized life, his conversion could not be considered complete or permanent. The mission was regarded as a temporary agency; once the Indian absorbed the ways of civilized man, he was to take his place in organized Spanish society, and the missionaries were to move on to new frontiers or become parish priests. As soon as the process of Christianization and civilization was completed in any one area, the mission lands, since they belonged collectively to the natives, were to be distributed among the Indians. When the system was originally established, it was assumed that the transition period would take about ten years, after which the Indians would be ready to take their place as Spanish subjects. In practice, however—particularly in colonial Mexico, or New Spain as it was called—the Spanish Padres found it necessary to continue their control over the Indians for an extended period of time.

The center of a Spanish mission was the Church, which was always the most ornate building. Various other buildings were also needed: they usually included a residence for the missionaries, houses for the Indians, workshops for carpenters, blacksmiths, and tailors; there was the all-important granary; there were store-rooms, kilns, shops, and all was enclosed by walls generally in the shape of a quadrangle, fortified at the gates or entrances. Outside the enclosure the agricultural fields were located, and beyond the fields in many cases there were supporting ranches. Each mission was a complete religious, economic, and social unit under the supervision of missionaries.

During their long history of colonization, the Spanish authorities learned that the mission was the most effective agency for controlling the frontier, and that clergymen, comparatively free from personal ambitions, were the most acceptable and successful agents on the frontier. As long as the Indians lived in the missions, their loyalty to Spain was assured and the problem of conquest by aggressive foreign nations was lessened.

Missionary work in Texas was entrusted to the Franciscan Padres, whose extensive activities in colonial Mexico had been remarkable. The Franciscans operated out of religious centers in Mexico, where missionaries were trained. Two of these centers, the College of Santa Cruz de Querétaro and the College of Zacatecas, furnished practically all the missionary manpower for Texas. The work was divided between the two colleges and each was responsible for specifically assigned missions, which for administrative purposes were identified as either Querétaran or Zacatecan missions.

The missionaries were primary agents in the transformation of a large part of the native population from a roving to a sedentary life. Spain considered the Indian worth civilizing and believed that he had to be converted and instructed in the faith if he was to become a useful member of society. The missionaries were effective collaborators in carrying out Spanish policy. They did not limit their activities to caring for the spiritual needs of the Indian. Their views on frontier matters, including international policy, helped form the opinions of central officials. Thus the instructions which came out of Mexico—or Spain itself in some cases—were both shaped and interpreted by the missionaries; for often they were the only ones who knew the conditions at first hand.

When the French tried to occupy the shores of Texas late in the seventeenth century, the Spaniards took energetic measures to occupy the region which they had always claimed as their own but had not settled or exploited. To win over the natives in East Texas, where the foreign danger was greatest, the Spaniards naturally used their most effective agency—the mission. Several missions were established and as long as the French danger continued the Spanish authorities spared no energy in supporting these institutions with protective *presidios* or garrisons.

Mission Nuestra Señora de la Purísma Concepción was established in East Texas near the Angelina River on July 7, 1716. About the same time the protective presidio of Nuestra Señora de los Dolores de los Tejas was established nearby. The area was inhabited by the friendly Hasani Indians and among other reasons was selected because it yielded a dependable source of maize, melons, beans, and tobacco. Mission Concepción—"de los Hasani" was the identifying specification added to the name—was only one of six missions established primarily to prevent French commercial expansion into the region. The early history of all these East Texas missions fluctuated with the international French-Spanish rivalry on the frontier. Official Spanish support was generous and sustained only as long as the French threatened, much to the chagrin of the missionaries who sincerely wanted to help these Indians. In 1719 all the missions in East Texas were temporarily abandoned. Two years later, however, renewed fear of French encroachments induced the Spanish authorities to re-establish them.

The history of Concepción Mission in the years that followed might be viewed as typical of the history of missions on the French-Spanish border. These were not thriving institutions; but they were cared for by dedicated Franciscan Padres, who were absorbed in religious work and who labored heroically in a difficult area, Christianizing, instructing, baptizing, and teaching the arts and crafts. In the ancient traditions of monastic life, their daily routine included the most menial tasks. They plowed, planted, and harvested; they cooked, washed, and mended clothes; they handled livestock; they served as nurses and doctors in the native huts; they built houses and churches. In East Texas the buildings were of the most flimsy character, and no trace of them remains.

Perhaps their hardest trial was loneliness, for they were educated men living among heathens who could not match or challenge them intellectually. They lived many leagues apart from their own kind, whom they visited only at long intervals. Missionary life was hard and called forth the highest qualities of manhood—character, dedication, courage, and endurance. Those who came willing to face martyrdom to spread the faith were denied this glorious crown and found their martyrdom in daily sacrifice, performing humble tasks for their fellow men.

After the French ceased to menace the Texas frontier, the problem of defense was simplified and the civil authorities withdrew some of their military support. Since the effective operation—even the existence—of the mission depended on military assistance, the Padres of the three Querétaran missions, having been deprived of protection and themselves doubting the possibility of making any headway with the Indians, asked the viceroy for permission to transfer their establishments to a more favorable location.

In selecting a site for the proposed transfer the Padres were naturally attracted to San Antonio; not only was it closer to the base of supplies in Mexico, but it was in the heart of an area where Indians were peaceful and friendly, where missionaries were being requested, and where military protection was assured. Furthermore, two successful missions were already in operation in San Antonio.

After protracted negotiations the Spanish authorities officially approved the missionaries' request to transfer three missions from East Texas to San Antonio: San Francisco de la Espada, San Juan Capistrano, and Purísima Concepción. In East Texas, Concepción Mission, since it was established specifically for the Hasani Indians, had been known by its full title "de los Hasani." The identifying phrase, meaningless in San Antonio, was changed to "de Acuña" in honor of the viceroy who authorized the transfer, the Marquéz de Casafuerte, whose name was Juan de Acuña.

All three missions were formally transferred on March 5, 1731, and established along the San Antonio River at easy distance from one another. In identical ceremonies the Indians' ownership of the land was recognized, the boundaries of each mission were clearly defined, and the rights to pasture lands and watering places established. Temporary structures of rough timber, roofed with grass, were erected as chapels; there were humble quarters for the Padres and crude shelters to store provisions and supplies for the Indians. Some of the Indians from East Texas, persuaded of the advantages of mission life, moved to San Antonio at the time of the transfer. It took a full month to move the missions to their new locations and to bring the Indians. The actual removal was no small feat. The distance covered was about 150 leagues, and all the moveable property of the missions—including not only the furnishings of the chapels, but the herds of cattle, horses, and burros—had to be transported.

The casual visitor viewing the ruins of any mission concludes that a mission was a church where Indians worshipped and were instructed. This limited view results in many misconceptions. Actually, a mission was an institution—a way of life, established in any area where Indians welcomed or accepted the missionaries; it was an agency for transmitting the Spanish language, culture, and manner of life to the natives. The Padres faced a difficult assignment which demanded not only heroic virtue but also a comprehensive knowledge of a variety of technical skills and an ever-present sympathetic understanding of the different cultural attitudes of their heathen charges. After the Indians were initiated into the ways of civilized men and could live in organized society with other Spanish subjects, the mission, having fulfilled its purpose, could be transferred elsewhere. Thus we can speak of the transfer of a mission without implying that the buildings were removed.

Transfer of the East Texas missions to San Antonio, however, meant that new buildings had to be erected, that fields had to be plowed and made ready for planting, that *acequias* or irrigation ditches had to be built, and that additional provisions had to be brought from the Rio Grande missions to feed the large number of Indians that were brought into organized community life. Three nations were now congregated: the Pacaos, the Pajalat, and the Alobja or Pitalaques. It has been estimated that one thousand Indians were gathered at the new missions. Three soldiers were stationed at each new establishment to help maintain order among the neophytes; at times the soldiers had to accompany the Padres in their journeys as they sought new recruits.

A total of five missions served the various Indian tribes gathered about San Antonio. In addition to the three transferred from East Texas in 1731, Mission San Antonio de Valero (The Alamo), established in 1718, and Mission San José de Aguayo, founded in 1720, were still in successful operation. Through most of the 18th Century these five missions thrived and the Indians prospered. As time passed and the Indians learned building skills, permanent structures of stone were erected, in keeping with the best architectural trends favored by the Spaniards. Fortifying walls were constructed to surround each mission. The remains of these structures, in various stages of preservation and repair, are the pride of San Antonio and an attraction for many tourists annually.

For the first several years after its transfer to San Antonio, Mission Concepción made material progress. Harvests were regularly gathered, and the various trades were successfully taught in the mission shops. The Franciscan Padres had reason to be satisfied with the spiritual progress as more and more Indians were baptized. Patient and persistent toil improved material conditions all around until a serious epidemic of smallpox broke out and spread to all five missions in 1739. Smallpox was a dreaded disease among the Indians, and many felt that their only safety was in flight. Only the heroic work of the missionaries prevented a complete exodus at this time. Losses from death and desertion were great. It is estimated that there were 250 Indians living in Concepción Mission before the epidemic; after it was over, there were only 120. Many of those who had fled in fear returned afterwards; others took the place of those who had died, and before long Concepción Mission could again boast of full quarters.

After this emergency, mission life quickly returned to the normal routine. The Padres instructed the neophytes twice a day, in the morning and the afternoon. Much time was spent in accumulating the food necessary to maintain the mission. Not only did the Indian have to be taught how to plant and harvest the crops, but irrigation ditches had to be constructed to assure a harvest. Surplus grain was exchanged for clothing, tobacco, and household utensils. The missionaries had medicine chests to take care of the sick and afflicted. The livestock had to be cared for so that the Indians could be supplied with meat. Occasionally the relentless Apaches had to be fought off; the sick and wounded had to be treated. Sometimes there were arguments with the civil authorities. There was wholesome recreation; religious and civic celebrations broke the monotony. The seasons passed, the Indians enjoyed peace and a measure of prosperity, and there was progress and expansion at Concepción Mission.

In 1745 Fray Francisco Xavier Ortiz came up from the College of Santa Cruz in Querétaro for an inspection of Concepción Mission. He reported that since its foundation in 1731 three hundred and ninety-three Indians had been baptized; two hundred and sixty-five had died and received the last sacraments; and at the time of his visitation sixty-two families, including two hundred and seven Indians, were living at the mission. Most of them were baptized Christians and thirty-one were being instructed in doctrine. He stated that a fine new permanent church was being built out of carved stone and that it was about half completed. An inventory of the mission showed that there were nine hundred head of cattle, three hundred sheep, and one hundred horses. There were thirty yoke of oxen, twenty hoes, forty axes, ten adzes, and all the necessary tools for complete blacksmith and carpenter shops, as well as for stone work and masonry.

Mission Concepción, as all fully developed missions, contained all that was necessary for a well-ordered and self-supporting unit. The missionary himself directed the activities; sometimes he was assisted by a lay brother who possessed special technical skills. To help supervise the labor of the Indians, keep them in order, punish minor offenses, or instruct in elementary tasks, native officers were appointed.

The successful cultivation of the fields depended in large measure on an ingenious irrigation system which brought water from the San Antonio River to the mission. A dam was built upstream and an *acequia*, variously known as Concepción ditch or Pajalache ditch, led the water down Garden Street—since known as South St. Mary's Street—in a direct line to Mission Concepción. Constructed soon after the mission was begun, the irrigation project carried water for well over a century. By a series of canals the Indians watered their crops and cattle, certain that they could count on successful harvests.

The church of Concepción Mission is generally regarded as the best preserved ruin of its kind in Texas today. The front faces almost due west; its twin towers and Moorish dome can be seen from afar. Its walls, forty-five inches thick, are made of adobe and small stones; only the sculptured parts, the cornices and the door frames are hewn out of large stones. The front walls and towers are plastered, and traces of frescoes can still be seen in places. Over the main entrance there is an arch on which the following carved inscription proclaims that the church is dedicated to the Immaculate Conception:

A SU PATRONA, Y PRINCESSA
CON ESTAS ARMAS, ATIENDE
ESTA MISSION, Y DEFIENDE
EL PUNTO DE SU PUREZA

Rendered in English the inscription reads: "This mission honors its patroness and princess and defends with these arms the doctrine of her purity."

The main altar was adorned with a statue of the Immaculate Conception, excellently carved and enhanced with a silver crown. The present altar and its decorations, the communion rail, and the benches are all comparatively modern. In the side chapels were statues of Our Lady of Sorrows and of Our Lady of the Pillar. There was an altar likewise in each of the rooms under the towers. In the one which served as a baptistry, the font, though considerably deteriorated by the destructive action of time and perhaps even mutilated by vandals, is still to be seen; it consists of an artistically carved symbolic figure, with outstretched arms supporting the bowl into which the water was poured. In this room the walls also bear traces of frescoing: the outline of a crucifixion scene is still visible above the baptismal font.

An interesting feature is the stone stairway—approached from either the sacristy or the yard—leading to what was evidently the infirmary, but the walls above show extensive crumbling, and much of the stairway is now in ruins. Another stone stairway is to be seen above the baptistry, leading to the look-out windows in the tower above.

The monastery which adjoined the church is now partly in ruins. With its arched porticoes it no doubt presented a beautiful spectacle from the plaza side, but the arches have at some time or other been filled in and the openings fitted with modern windows; its architectural value has, therefore, been almost entirely lost.

The Padres directing the affairs of Mission Concepción were brought into direct contact with the civil authorities in San Antonio. The decrees of various Spanish officials, promulgated from time to time, delineated the authority and responsibilities of the religious, civilian, and military authorities. There was to be mutual cooperation, since the frontier lands of the King of Spain could not develop and prosper without it. While harmony often prevailed, it was not unusual—particularly in dealings with unsympathetic local authorities—for the Padres to defend vigorously their own rights as missionaries and to uphold the rights given to the Indians by Spanish law.

Under the direction of the Franciscans, Mission Concepción—and the same can be said about the neighboring missions—experienced a degree of material and spiritual progress which at times was in striking contrast to the wretched and precarious existence of the civil settlers living in the city. Undoubtedly this was

largely the result of the intelligent and disinterested
direction of a remarkable group of missionaries who
achieved their goal by slow degrees and by sustained
and persistent effort. Those civilian settlers who failed
to display the industrious habits of responsible men
looked upon the relatively prosperous missions with
deep resentment. Worse, they unscrupulously stole mission cattle, helped themselves to the produce of the cultivated fields of the Indians, and were guilty of various
minor violations. Naturally the missionaries protested.

It is true that some of the conflicts were jurisdictional, and often heightened by personality clashes. Thus,
shortly after Governor Don Carlos Benites Franquis de
Lugo arrived in Texas in 1736, he ordered the withdrawal of two of the three soldiers stationed at each of the
missions, Concepción, San Francisco de la Espada, and
San Juan Capistrano, stating that they were needed for
duty at the *presidio*. The Padres depended on the services of the soldiers not only to maintain order among
the Indians but also to assist in many of the routine jobs
of operating the mission. Actually soldiers were indis-
pensable when the Padres had to pursue runaway Indians. Naturally the missionaries protested and objected to the Governor's order. Thus began a long controversy which was soon extended to other jurisdictional
questions, including the charge that the Governor intercepted the mail when the missionaries appealed to higher authority. Abusive language on the part of the Governor increased the ill feeling already existing. The
question of returning the mission guards was not settled until the viceroy, acting on the formal protests of
the Padres who demonstrated that the spiritual and
temporal welfare of the missions was in jeopardy, ordered Governor Franquis to restore the guards previously stationed at the missions. The Governor, demon-
strating an independence not often witnessed in Spanish
colonial administration, advanced reasons why he refused to comply with the order. The dispute continued
until Franquis, also charged with other violations, was

removed from office. Subsequently the guards were restored.

From time to time visitors or inspectors toured the Texas missions to examine conditions at first hand. Sometimes, as a substitute, they called for detailed written reports from the missionaries. In response to a request from his superiors, Padre Francisco de los Dolores, administrator of Mission Concepción, submitted a detailed report concerning the status of the mission in 1762. This important document has frequently been consulted and quoted by historians. Dr. Carlos Casteñeda, who spent a large part of his life studying and writing about the missions, gives the following description of Mission Concepción on the basis of the report of Padre Dolores.

"Its church, which had now been completed, was thirty-two *varas* long and eight *varas* wide, built of stone with a dome. It had two towers with bells. Above the main altar there was a fresco of the *Cinco Senores*. Its tabernacle was gilded, and over the main altar, in an oval shaped niche, was an elegantly sculptured image in honor of Our Lady of Sorrows and Our Lady of the Pillar. The church was furnished with two confessionals, several benches and a pulpit. Beneath the two towers there were two small chapels: one dedicated to Saint Michael, with a very pleasing altar, and the other used as a baptistry. Here there was a baptismal font of copper with its cover, three anointers, and a silver shell.

"The sacristy was a room with an arched ceiling twelve *varas* square and was fitted with closets and drawers, where three chalices with their patens were kept, together with a ciborium, cruets, a tray, and a censer, all made of silver. There were also several missals, twelve complete sets of vestments made of Persian silk and ten of damask, three copes, a good supply of altar cloths and various ornaments for the celebration of the different feasts of the Church.

"The friary had the necessary cells for the missionaries and other rooms for offices and storage. It was one-story high with a pleasing archway along the side. All the rooms and cells were decorated with good taste. Adjoining the living quarters of the missionaries was a large hall, where the looms of the mission were installed. It also had two storerooms. Here woolen and cotton cloth of various kinds were woven for the use of the mission inmates. Blankets, too, were made here. In the adjoining storerooms the wool and cotton used were also stored together with the combs, cards, spinning wheels and other equipment. The granary was in a separate building, where sixteen hundred bushels of corn and one hundred bushels of beans were kept.

"For the cultivation of the fields the mission had forty-five yokes of oxen and the necessary number of plows, plowshares, hoes, and other tools. Its blacksmith shop was fully equipped with its anvil, bellows, hammers, tongs, and sledge hammers. The mission was also well provided with all the tools necessary for carpentry and cabinet making, which were used by the Indians in keeping their houses and the entire mission property in repair and in making furniture required for their needs.

"The Indian pueblo proper was arranged in two tiers of stone houses on either side of the church and monastery, all enclosed within a rectangular wall for its protection. Each Indian family was provided with the necessary pots and pans, its grindstone for corn, and a flat iron for cooking their tortillas (corn cakes) over the coals. The cultivated fields were fenced and irrigated by a ditch that led the water from the river, where a stone dam had been built. The mission owned a ranch, where it had several houses for the caretakers who looked after the two hundred mares, one hundred and twenty horses, six hundred and ten head of cattle, and twenty-two hundred sheep and goats.

"According to the records of the mission it had baptized seven hundred and ninety-two persons since its establishment, of whom five hundred and fifty-eight had been given Christian burial. At this time there were fifty-eight families living in the mission, who together with the orphans and widows, made a total of two hundred and seven persons of both sexes and all ages."

The report of Padre Dolores describes conditions at Mission Concepción at a time when it was prospering under the management of the Padres from the College of Santa Cruz in Querétaro. It was the Querétaran Fathers who originally founded the mission in 1716 and supervised its transfer to San Antonio in 1731. They labored at a great many mission establishments located at various strategic frontier points in Texas and made heroic contributions while pacifying and developing the frontier. Eventually, however, circumstances forced them to transfer control of their missions to the Padres from the College of Zacatecas.

When the Jesuits were expelled from all the Spanish colonies in 1767, they vacated important and thriving spiritual posts, well provided with permanent churches which had been cared for by Jesuit missionaries. To solve the problem of replacement, the viceroy, after conferring with Franciscan authorities and receiving their consent, issued a formal decree on July 28, 1772, withdrawing the Querétaran Padres from Mission Concepción as well as from all their other works in the Province of Texas, and turning over the management and operation of their works to the missionaries from the College of Zacatecas. The actual transfer took place early in 1773 under the supervision of Governor Ripperdá, and was carried out in a very business-like manner after certified copies of the inventories were exchanged. After departing from Texas, the Querétarans extended their activities to California.

No substantial changes occurred at Mission Concepción after the Zacatecan Padres accepted the responsibility of management. None were expected, since the missionaries from both colleges were members of the Franciscan Order, imbued with the same spirit and possessing the same dedication. The Zacatecan missionaries zealously carried on and Mission Concepción experienced continued growth.

When Mission Concepción was transferred to San Antonio in 1731, it was generally believed that Christianizing and civilizing the Indians would take about ten years. After the mission accomplished its prime purpose, communal living under supervision would be terminated, and hopefully the Indians would join well organized communities and assume the responsibilities of ordinary citizens. The act of dividing and distributing the properties of the mission, called secularization, consisted of distributing all the moveable properties and surplus products as well as the livestock and agricultural lands which had been cultivated and held in common during the formation period. These properties were to be divided equitably among the Indians, who were then expected to take their place in a civilized community living under the laws of Spain.

When secularization took place, the church buildings and living quarters of the Padres were turned over to the Bishop, along with all the ornaments, sacred vestments, and other church property. The administration of these properties became the direct responsibility of the Bishop. If circumstances warranted, he would create a parish and appoint a priest to minister to the spiritual needs of all who came within the territorial limits of the new parish unit. It should be emphasized that the parish priest did not have the all-inclusive powers of a missionary Padre. Secularization meant, therefore, that the mission as an institution or as a way of life disappeared.

Secularization of the San Antonio missions had been contemplated for many years before it actually took place, but for one reason or another the step was always delayed. The royal authorities believed that financing the missions of Texas drained too much wealth from the royal treasury, and tried to hasten secularization. In fact as time passed some of the Padres, notably Padre Manuel Silva, urged a reorganization of some and a secularization of others. The problem in Texas was complicated because the primitive stage of mission life permitted a continual renewal or addition of uncivilized Indians, generation after generation. Under these conditions it was difficult to establish a terminal point at which secularization should take place. The Spanish officials continued to study the question until the Commandante General of the Interior Provinces, Don Pedro de Nava issued a decree on April 10, 1794, ordering the secularization of most of the missions in Texas and outlining the procedure for distributing personal property and communal property.

A critical examination of the instructions given to Governor Muñoz, of the precise directions for carrying them out, and of the inventory of all the temporal possessions of the missions, will reveal not only some interesting facts about secularization but will likewise furnish an insight into Spanish colonial procedures. The directives illustrate that the higher Spanish officials recognized that minor officials and ordinary citizens would be tempted to exploit the Indians after they were removed from the protective custody of the Padres; they also demonstrate that Spanish policy demanded justice for the Indians.

There are fifteen numbered articles containing explicit statements of policy, which set forth the Spanish concept of secularization. These articles, too lengthy to be quoted in full, can be excerpted as follows:

"1. That the old method of community property which has been followed and observed in the administration of the temporal possessions of the natives, be reformed and henceforth abolished . . .

"2. That the old methods be continued only in the new acquisitions . . . and in . . . the missions . . . [existing less than] ten years. . . .

"3. That in the old settlements and towns the Indian be given the very same freedom that the Spaniards enjoy, and which the laws and other ordinances allow, so that they may tend their own cattle, prepare and till their lands, avail themselves of the animals they raise and of their crops, apply themselves to the trades, profits and industries that they may like best, and serve or work for hire in order to support and clothe their families; and the magistrates must watch and exercise special care over them, that they may not live in idleness, indulge in improper amusements, get drunk, or fall into any other excesses to which they are inclined.

"4. That the magistrates diligently see to it that the Indians be paid for their productions at just prices, as well as the accustomed salaries or wages, or whatever salaries or wages they may have stipulated with their employers, in ready money, according to schedule and instructions . . .

"5. That professional gamblers be forbidden to enter their towns as well as barterers who introduce into them wines, spirituous drinks and other liquors; for besides promoting the vice of drunkenness, . . . they extort from them in exchange and at lowest prices, the cattle, productions and seeds that they need for the support of their families, thus leaving them in danger of perishing from want, or compelling them to steal or resort to some other objectionable means of obtaining their livelihood.

"6. That the best and most fertile lands adjacent to every settlement be separated and used as its community property . . .

"7. That the remaining lands be distributed among the Indians in *suertes* [each *suerte* or plat 400 *varas* long and 200 *varas* wide]. . . . The aforementioned *suertes* must be subdivided so that everybody may have his proportionate and just share.

"8. That they may be given warranties or titles of ownership, specifying the dimensions and boundaries of the lands to them apportioned; and same are given them in the name of the king in perpetuity, unto them, their children and descendants, under the binding condition of maintaining their houses and families in the town, of not conveying them, mortgaging them, or casting upon them any shadow whatever, not even with a pious motive, and they must keep them under cultivation and in good value; and he incurs the penalty of losing them who abandons them for two years, after which time they may be given to a more industrious and deserving man.

"9. That excepting the *caciques* [Indian chiefs], generals, their lieutenants, and the governors and justices of each town, the other Indians are under obligation of working in common, of preparing and sowing in corn or some other seed adapted to the country the *suertes* set aside to their respective communities. . . . In case it is necessary for them to work more, either because greater sowings than usual are made or because the Indians are few or if they are required to herd the cattle, to serve as messengers, or to carry the products of the fields to other towns to sell for higher prices because of greater demand there, or if required to do any other duties, they must be paid their salaries or wages out of the community funds if they work in behalf of the community, and by private individuals who may hire them in the manner already prescribed . . .

"10. That the management and administration of the community property be faithfully observed hereafter, the rules specified by . . . the Ordinance on the Management in Districts, with the declarations, additions or changes that may have been made by royal orders, by resolutions of the supreme Council of the Exchequer and by the dispositions of His Excellency, the Viceroy. . . .

"11. That in accordance with the requirements of the Royal Ordinance on District Governors, the subdelegated Spaniards, who must be exercising official duties in the principal towns settled by the Indians only . . . enforce, as far as possible, the very same regulations in the direction and management of the lands and other property of their communities . . . as are prescribed for the public funds derived from public lands and excise taxes of the cities, towns and villages of Spaniards.

"12. That the said subdelegates take care that the Indians of each district or commonwealth cultivate the community lands, and if that is not done, they must see that all or part of said lands are rented or administered with their approval and that of their governors and justices, and that the products derived from them and from other community property after deducting expenses, be put in a chest with three keys, said chest to belong in the royal houses [town halls] of the head towns in which the aforementioned subdelegates reside or in some other perfectly safe place.

"13. That at the end of every year be made and sent to the central government an account of receipts and expenses, certifying by document or some other valid process that the Indian officials of the commonwealth were present in person . . . to learn of the good manner and fairness with which the products of their community property are handled, the governor or magistrate [*alcalde*] and the alderman [*regidor*] of longest standing among them must have in their possession two of the keys to the aforementioned chest, while the Spanish judge must retain the third.

"14. That the governor . . . take counsel for me with the

subdelegates of the head-towns among the Indians . . . that the protectors of the Indians . . . are required to be present at the meetings of said Board and the formation of the accounts, so that they may plead and ask for what they may think just and proper in behalf of the Indians over whom their jurisdiction extends . . .

"15. And finally . . . the clergymen in charge of the missions and the secular ecclesiastics who are serving as parish priests to the Indians are hereby relieved of the care and management of the temporal possessions of the towns they have had under their supervision until now, . . . the direction whereof the king's judges are henceforth charged in the terms already specified, and they must begin to exercise their duties in every place at once or as soon as they receive these resolutions, said property being delivered unto them under formal inventory."

April 10, 1794

Pedro de Nava, *Commandante General*,
Interior Provinces of New Spain

On receipt of the detailed directive, Governor Don Manuel Muñoz of Texas, on July 31 and August 1, 1794, proceeded to carry out the order insofar as it affected Mission Concepción. He personally presided over the ceremonies. Padre José María Camarena represented the missionaries, and Don Pedro Huisar surveyed the shares to be partitioned. The Indians were represented by their Chief, the Spanish *alcalde* was represented by his son Polinario Gil, and most of the Indians from Mission Concepción were there in person.

After a formal reading of the pertinent official documents—a routine Spanish formality—the proceedings got underway. The official list showed that there were sixteen men, twelve married women, three widows, one boy, and six girls, making a total of thirty-eight persons living at the mission. The lands were surveyed as stipulated and eight *suertes* (each plat 400 by 200 *varas*) were set aside for common use. An additional eighteen *suertes* were surveyed and distributed as follows: sixteen to the Indians from the mission, one to Xavier Longoria who was charged with directing and supervising the agricultural activities of the common lands, and one *suerte* to the Spanish *alcalde* since he was to receive no salary for directing the Indians, keeping their funds, and assuming the responsibility for community development.

The Indians were then given their other personal property which had formerly been controlled by the missionaries. The inventory of these properties was detailed and precise. These included cattle, saddle horses, hogs, plows, hoes, tongs, saws, axes, planes, chisels, mason's trowels, grinding stones, etc. There were also large supplies of consumable goods such as unthreshed wheat. All these properties were ceremoniously distributed and apportioned among the Indians. They were also given the quarters in which they had been living "all of which are within a stone wall with three gates, one having a peep-window and all provided with locks."

Secularization also meant that every mission Indian was given all the liberty, freedom, and privileges granted by law to Spaniards. Accordingly, they were permitted to engage freely in trade, pursuing the works they preferred, or they could seek gainful employment as laborers. Public officials were to be particularly zealous in protecting the interests of the Indian. Unfortunately, as it turned out, the Indian, while enjoying theoretical liberty, did not actually enjoy as much freedom as the law provided. The civil officials, devoid of the serious interest in the Indians' welfare that had characterized the devoted missionaries, often exploited them. Thus even though the law specified that the Indians were to be given specific wages when they worked as laborers, unprincipled officials often paid ridiculously low prices for products and labor.

It became apparent as the years rolled on that the secularization decree was not meeting the expectations of those who had ordered it. Some of the Indians continued to live in their houses within the mission walls and tried to cultivate their lands; others drifted away. Most were shiftless, and the annual yield fell far below that of the days when solicitous missionaries carefully supervised the work of the Indians. The end of all organized life at Mission Concepción was in sight under such circumstances.

When visitors at Mission Concepción view the silent ruins of a bygone civilization, they are apt to conclude what has unfortunately been concluded by other visitors and even by some writers, that the missions in Texas were grand failures. This conclusion is based on a failure to understand the Spanish colonial system. The missions were established as temporary frontier posts, they were not meant to be permanent institutions; they were instruments for training the Indians for civilized living according to Christian principles. They served their purpose even gloriously and contributed to the growth of Spanish civilization in Texas. Neither Concepción Mission or the other Texas missions failed, but their successors failed in large measure to build upon the foundation which had been established.

After the turn of the century and after the last mission-trained Indians drifted away, Mission Concepción was practically deserted. Squatters moved in and out, various individuals plundered, and even vandals had their day.

Anglo-American settlers moved into Texas in ever-increasing numbers after the new colonization laws permitted them to do so. They bought choice lands which were not expensive. The lands surrounding the old missions were not available, however, and it was generally conceded that this was church property and had a special character. Nevertheless, with the passing of time various individuals tried to acquire some of the lands and even the mission buildings. In 1822 applications for the lands of Mission Concepción were made by several Spanish families. Various petitions, including one for the sale of the stone and rock in the walls and buildings were sent to the Governor. The decision on the sale of the lands and buildings was referred to the State Legislature in August 1825. A long controversy followed as the subject was alternately approved, opposed, and suspended. A period of uncertainty and confusion followed which delayed the sale. Nevertheless debate on the question prompted prospective occupants or future owners to move on the abandoned lands. By 1829 fifty families established themselves in and around Mission Concepción. Finally in 1831 the uncertainty of what could be sold was terminated when a decree ordered the sale at public auction for cash of all Mission Concepción properties except the Church. There were some who objected to the entire proceedings and disapproved of the final decision.

The rights of the Catholic Church to the mission properties—some of which were again abandoned after the Texas Revolution—were formally and officially acknowledged when the legislature of the Republic of Texas on January 13, 1841, passed an act declaring that Mission Concepción, along with all the San Antonio missions and other specified Texas missions and the lands immediately surrounding them—not to exceed fifteen acres—as the property "of the present chief pastor of the Roman Catholic Church, in the Republic of Texas, and his successors in office, in trust forever."

Bishop John Mary Odin, "the chief pastor" and the legal owner of all mission properties in his diocese, felt that the future of the Catholic Church in San Antonio depended on its educational institutions. To secure good teachers he journeyed to France and successfully negotiated with the Society of Mary for the services of Brothers to open a school in San Antonio. The Bishop not only financed the trip of the Brothers to Texas, but also bore the whole cost of erecting and providing for the school. He, however, announced his intention of turning the entire undertaking over to the Brothers as soon as it should become self-sustaining.

Begun in 1852 as a small day and boarding school, and known as St. Mary's School, the new institution was soon beset with its normal share of difficulties. That the school should expand—it eventually developed into the present St. Mary's University—and that other sustaining properties should be acquired, particularly farm lands, had always been the cherished hope of Brother Andrew Edel, its first principal. Since tuition fees were small, the Brothers could manage much easier, Edel believed, if they acquired farms on which produce of all kinds could be raised to help sustain the school. Bishop Odin came to the rescue and gave them the use of the lands of Mission Concepción some time before the end of February, 1855.

Meanwhile, Father Leo Meyer, the Provincial Superior of all the Brothers residing in America, not entirely satisfied with conditions at the school in San Antonio, proposed to close the institution and transfer the Brothers to other establishments. Bishop Odin, considerably disturbed, made his countermove. The time had arrived, he stated, for the Brothers to take over completely the management of the school; he proposed to arrange the transfer of property titles with Father Meyer. He stated that he intended to give the Brothers "as a gift" the entire property of Mission Concepción on which "if the soil be well cultivated, more corn and vegetables could be raised than a large community could consume." He suggested that Brother Edel be given charge of the mission and farm so that he could establish there some type of manual training school at which the orphans of the surrounding country could be cared for and educated. This would of course necessitate the appointment of another superior for the city school, but Edel, whose "considerable skill in agriculture" would make him invaluable at the new establishment, should by all means be put in charge. The Bishop was eager to complete the transfer of properties and terminate all ideas of withdrawing the Brothers and bringing his labors of several years as well as his plans for the future to an abrupt ending.

As finally drawn up on September 8, 1859, the contract was made between the Most Reverend John M. Odin and Brother Andrew M. Edel, and their heirs and successors forever. The contract stipulated that the Brothers of Mary obligated themselves to keep forever in the city of San Antonio and on the premises then occupied, a school for the instruction of youth. Secondly, it obliged Bishop Odin on his part to transfer and convey to the Brothers the schoolhouse, dependencies, and land occupied as St. Mary's School and also the mission buildings and land of Mission Concepción, with the provision that the Brothers could not in any way alienate or encumber the properties. The land was to be theirs in perpetuity provided that they continued to maintain the school.

After obtaining a clear title to the Mission Concepción property, the Brothers set about restoring the church and improving the land; they even added to it by purchasing additional acreage. When all was in readiness, this ancient structure, which had been entirely abandoned as a religious institution for well over half a century, was again blessed and opened as a place of worship. Brother Edel thus described the event:

> "On Tuesday, May 28, 1861 early in the morning, we left in procession with banners and flags and the statue of the Blessed Virgin richly ornamented, carried by our students, who were decorated with silk red and light-blue sashes tipped with gold tassels. All of our students were in the procession; also a large number of little girls dressed in white, many parents, and a crowd of people. Father Amandus celebrated Mass, and Msgr. Madrid preached, as did also Fathers Faure and Amandus. Our students sang during Mass. We spent the entire day at the Mission and before leaving sang several hymns in honor of the Blessed Virgin. At noon, we furnished refreshments to all the school children and to others who so desired, Brother Lawrence had baked about a thousand cakes and peach pies. Everything was eaten. It was a day of joy and pleasure for all. Father Faure intends to say Mass there from time to time on Thursdays. We will probably go there next Thursday with the students."

For several years during the early 1860's the Society of Mary used Mission Concepción for training its candidates. It conducted there a postulate and novitiate under the direction of Brother Paul Kraus. Ten to fifteen young men were admitted as candidates. The whole project for training candidates was begun prematurely, was never entirely successful, and was terminated in 1866 when the remaining candidates were sent to the Provincial motherhouse in Dayton, Ohio, to complete their teacher training.

Even after the novitiate was closed, Brother Edel and a few assistants continued in residence and worked the land until 1869 when the farm was closed and leased for cultivation to Joseph Keller. Subsequently Messrs. Koenig, Ross, Brackenridge, Hank, and Haechten in turn held leases on the property, but of course had no control of the buildings of Mission Concepción.

Before the land was rented, the practice of bringing the boarding students from the downtown school to spend part of the summer at the mission was started and continued for years. The boarding students, who came from great distances, often spent their vacation at the school. During the hottest part of the summer they were transferred to the mission property where, along with the faculty, in pleasing and healthful environs they were given an opportunity for swimming, fishing, and hunting along the picturesque San Antonio River. The arrangement suggested a European summer "villa." Long after the practice was discontinued, the Brothers spent some of their more pleasant hours at the mission. Apart from the students, away from the cares of the classroom, and among themselves amidst pleasant surroundings they passed many restful hours.

About the end of the century there were many changes. The boarders were given new and spacious quarters of their own on a separate campus in the western part of the city. There were new educational problems. The city was growing, and the cares of the Bishop of San Antonio multiplied. It was a time for re-examination and reorganization. In 1911, at the request of Bishop Shaw, the Society of Mary gave Mission Concepción and the surrounding property to the Bishop of San Antonio and in return received unencumbered title to St. Mary's College located in downtown San Antonio.

Soon after the transfer of title, the Bishop built an orphanage on the mission grounds. Subsequently, in 1919, Bishop Drossaerts began building a seminary for the diocese. The grounds, originally set aside to serve as a center for converting heathen Indians have since become a focal point for training priests, modern missionaries who spread the gospel in a modern world, carrying on the traditions to which Mission Concepción was originally dedicated.

San Francisco de Espada

Mission San Francisco de Espada

San Francisco de Espada

by

Dorman H. Winfrey

The varied geographical locations in the history of the San Francisco de la Espada Mission suggest the turmoil of the mission era.

San Francisco de la Espada Mission was established in 1690 as the first East Texas mission of San Francisco de los Tejas, just west of the Neches River near present-day Weches in Houston County; re-established as Nuestro Padre San Francisco de los Neches in 1716; relocated six miles west of present Alto in Cherokee County and re-established in 1721 as San Francisco de los Neches; removed in 1730 to the Colorado River in the vicinity of present Zilker Park at Austin; and the following year moved to its final location in San Antonio on the San Antonio River and renamed San Francisco de la Espada.

It was born in fear and nurtured in conflict. When the French explorer, Robert Cavelier, Sieur de La Salle, landed on Matagorda Bay in February, 1785, Spanish fears of a foreign aggressor prompted the establishment of the mission. Although La Salle's expedition failed, and he was killed, the Spanish dared not risk having the land north of the Rio Grande fall into French hands. Spanish expeditions were dispatched to Texas. One of these, under Governor Alonso de León, reached the ruins of La Salle's Fort Saint Louis on April 22, 1689. When De León returned to Mexico, he reported favorably on the Texas region and recommended more attention be paid to the country and people. His report set in motion the events that would culminate in the mission's establishment.

In March of the next year, De León left Monclova with an expedition including Father Domian Massanet and three other Franciscan priests of the College of Santa Cruz de Querétaro, and a military escort of more than one hundred men. On May 25th, the party arrived at a wooded location on the Neches River and found friendly Indians and fields of corn, beans and melons. Under spreading pine, hickory, and oak, the Spaniards sang the *Te Deum Landamus*, said high mass, and began preparations for building a mission dedicated to Saint Francis of Assisi.

With the assistance of the amiable Indians, the Spaniards constructed the small, wooden mission. The eager willingness of the Indians was prompted, according to early accounts, by their fascination with the church bell. They soon learned the tolling bell at early dawn and in the dusk of twilight meant a call to prayer and certain frantic ringings of the bell warned of trouble.

These Indians, fascinated by a bell, were the Tejas tribe (meaning friends and allies) who gave their name to Texas. Four hundred miles from the nearest Spanish settlement and eighty-six years before the American Revolution would forerun a new nation, they toiled beside the Franciscans.

De León wanted to leave a protective garrison of fifty soldiers with the priests at the mission when he departed, but the Indian chieftain objected to the presence of so many unmarried men, and only three soldiers remained. Father Massanet and the military expedition returned to Mexico. The priests left behind said their farewell, according to Father Massanet's account, "with tears of joy and gladness, for these men did not sorrow at being left behind; nay rather, they gave thanks to God for having merited such a grace as to be called to save the souls of the heathen."

When Massanet returned to Texas in 1691 with the expedition of Domingo Terán de los Rios, he found the previously joyous priests facing severe hardships. Disease had killed one missionary and many Indians. Nature destroyed the crops with floods, then inflicted severe drought. The Indians rejected the missionaries and refused to be congregated. Father Massanet sadly concluded the Tejas Indians did not want to be Christianized and did not like the Spaniards. He also decided mission success would require establishment of regular presidios and careful selection of suitable sites.

Conditions did not improve, and by the fall of 1693, the Indian hostility became openly brazen. The Spaniards were forced to abandon San Francisco de los Tejas. Father Massanet recorded his description of preparations to leave: "Secretly the valuable ornaments were packed, the heavier articles, such as cannon, bells, and other things of similar nature were buried, and when everything was in readiness, on October 25, 1693, fire was applied to the Mission San Francisco de los Tejas, founded with so many sacrifices and so much expense." The end of this mission experience was in sharp contrast to its cordial beginning in May, 1690.

Re-establishment of the first East Texas mission was prompted again in 1715 by fear of the French. A Frenchman, Louis Juchereau de Saint Denis, arrived in Texas to promote trade. Another Spanish expedition was mounted for East Texas. Domingo Ramón, the leader of the next expedition, had orders to halt the French invader and suppress his effort to maintain trade lines. As part of his endeavors, Ramón re-established the first East Texas mission. The new mission, Nuestro Padre San Francisco de los Tejas, was constructed about four leagues east of the location which had been forsaken twenty-two years before.

Placed in charge of the mission were Fray Francisco Hidalgo, who had been on the expedition with Father Massanet and remained at San Francisco de los Tejas until the withdrawal in 1693, and Fray Isidro Félix de Espinosa, who also helped to establish two other missions in East Texas. In 1719 when the French invaded East Texas from Louisiana, Nuestro Padre San Francisco de los Tejas Mission was also abandoned.

Spain was faced with the task of recovering the East

Texas area. The Marquis de Aguayo embarked on an expedition in 1721. While in East Texas, he re-established six missions, including Nuestro Padre San Francisco de los Tejas, which was relocated east of the Neches River, six miles west of present Alto in Cherokee County, and given the name San Francisco de los Neches Mission. Carlos E. Castañeda in his *Our Catholic Heritage in Texas* described this scene that took place on August 5th: "The eight companies of the battalion of San Miguel de Aragón were drawn up in military formation . . . before the temporary church which had been hurriedly built for the occasion. High mass was sung with all solemnity by the Reverend Father Antonio Margil de Jesús and a salute fired by the troops at the proper time. The bells pealed a joyous welcome to the amazed Indians who came in great numbers to witness the ceremony while the trumpets blew and the drums rolled."

Another move came when, in 1730, the Spanish decided to close the mission. The now peaceful attitude of the Indians and the economic hardship of maintaining a presidio in such a distant location, dictated the fate of Nuestra Señora de los Delores de los Tejas. After the presidio had been abolished, the missionaries of San Francisco de los Neches requested relocation and were moved to a site on the Colorado River near the present location of Austin's Zilker Park.

The mission experiment had been costly and painful, but also valuable to the Spaniards. The country had been explored, clearer knowledge of its geography had been obtained—rivers named and charted, and roads to aid settlement later, marked out. And in the eyes of the dedicated priests Christianity had been brought to some of the heathen. Historian Robert Carlton Clark paid this tribute: "The zeal which conceived this missionary establishment in the midst of an unexplored wilderness, the self-sacrificing spirit of the holy men who undertook the well-nigh hopeless task of bringing the savage children of the forest to know and respond to the better impulses of the Christian religion are worthy of the highest commendation."

Finally on March 5, 1731, the cornerstone of the fourth and final location of the mission of San Francisco de la Espada was laid at the present site on the San Antonio River, some five miles southeast of the city of San Antonio. The location away from tourist routes has decreased the number of its visitors but not its vital historical importance.

Every area of its origin and history abounds with significant facts. Its name is an interesting starting point. The first part of the title refers to St. Francis of Assisi, the Founder of the Franciscan Order, to whom the mission is dedicated. The second part "de la Espada" has several interpretations. Honor was bestowed often on a Spanish grandee or a particular Spanish locality. In this instance, it is believed the person honored had the title of Duke of Espada. A more hypothetical interpretation suggests the word "espada" (sword) describes the sword-hilt design of the bell tower on the church.

The name, although long, was much shorter than the never ending work day of the priests. In theory the mission was established to convert the savage Indians to Christianity. Purely missionary tasks, however, occupied only a small part of the priests' time. In order to convert the Indians to a different mode of life, the Padres instructed the Indians in agriculture, stock raising, and crafts.

The Indians received Christian doctrine instruction twice a day, and explanation of the mysteries of the faith three or four times a week. Each morning before work, and each evening after work, all the Indians recited in concert the text of the Christian Doctrine. Although the ambitions of the padres were lofty, the achievements were meager. One of the most defeating obstacles to missionary education of the Indians was the language barrier. Although the zealous Padres studied the principal language of the nearby tribes, the tongues were so difficult and numerous the frustrated priests resorted to sign languages. It was this educational handicap that prompted Padre Bartholomé Garcia, the missionary at Espada in 1760, to compose a manual in both Spanish and Indian. This book, containing all that was essential to the administration of the sacraments of Baptism, Holy Eucharist, Extreme Unction, and Matrimony, was of invaluable assistance to his co-workers and successors. The manual, first published in Mexico in 1760, was intended for tribes in the vicinity of the San Antonio missions. The title page lists eighteen Indian tribes to which it is specifically addressed: Pajalates, Orejones, Pacaos, Pacóas, Tilijayas, Alasapas, Pausanes, Pauaches, Mescales, Pampopas, Tacames, Chayopines, Venados, Pamaques, Pihuiques, Borados, Sanipaos, and Manos de Perro.

A description of the original form of the mission is almost as difficult as the mastery of the tongues of its Indian converts. The Mission of San Francisco de la Espada has undergone innumerable alterations and destructions. Originally, it was similar to others, however, for it had a chapel, granary, monks' home, Indians' home, forts, plaza, land for grazing stock, and a mission well.

The chapel was initially built in the form of a cross. It was small; the frontage was twenty-four feet. The front wall, forty-five inches thick, supported the belfry with its three bells. At the summit of the belfry today is a beautifully wrought iron cross. The entrance to the chapel is Moorish in design.

By 1745 a new church of stone and mortar was underway. The sacristy had already been finished and was being used as the place for divine worship. Above the modest altar was an image of Saint Francis, carved in relief. On either side were two pictures, San Bernadino and San Juan Capistrano. All the sacred vessels and other ornaments were of silver. Although eventual completion of the church was planned, the structure remained untouched for many years. The Indians worked slowly and irregularly at their various mission tasks. They were not accustomed to sustained effort and their aversion to systematic labor had to be overcome with patience.

The general plan included a convent with four cells on the second story, and three on the ground floor plus their corridors, a workshop and a spacious granary, all of stone. In the cells were the necessary utensils and furnishings for the Indians.

The granary, built of stone and mortar, was a large and spacious building. In 1762 over two thousand bushels of corn, one hundred bushels of beans, and a good supply of chili, salt, cotton and wool were stored here for the use of the mission Indians. To cultivate the fields there were thirty-seven yokes of oxen, forty harrows, the necessary plows, fifty-eight hoes, forty-six axes, ten scythes, and sixteen bars. There were also necessary tools for carpentry, masonry, and black-smithing.

In order to maintain an independent life the mission owned a ranch outside the mission walls. It was here that cattle and stock were kept and cared for by ranch hands who lived on the premises. In the early years of the mission the stock consisted of 1,150 head of cattle, 740 sheep, ninety goats, and eighty-one horses for herding. Like the other missions, Espada had its own branding iron for its livestock.

One of the most interesting features of the mission is its aqueduct. Although the river is located nearby, its bed is so deep at this point that the water is not available for irrigation. Since the control and use of water is vital to the life of a mission, the Padres had to devise a method by which water could be transported. Irrigation enabled the Friars to raise crops, and the crops attracted and held the Indians for the mission. In 1740 work was begun on an aqueduct and completed five years later. The water had to be drawn from the San Antonio River half a league away and transported past the obstacle of the Piedra Creek. The missionaries mastered this engineering problem to build an aqueduct, which is still in good condition today, and the only Spanish aqueduct in the United States. It has been said that the good friars made use of the method of teaching the neophytes that not by faith alone, but by work along with faith they would be saved. The aqueduct is still used for the transfer of water and may be seen to the east of the road about a mile north of the mission.

Originally there were four bulwarks, one at each corner of the mission. The structure of the mission served a dual purpose: it created an enclosed city in which the Indians could work, learn, and raise their families; and it provided protection from those Indians still uncivilized. Holes were drilled in the fort walls to provide outlets for muskets and cannons. The low door leading into the fort and to the adjoining buildings prevented hostile Indians from making effective use of their bows and arrows.

Construction of the mission was dictated by the way of life and the struggle for survival. Life at the mission of San Francisco de la Espada was characteristic of the pattern of the mission era. The fluctuating fortunes of the period from 1731 to 1761, at the mission, paralleled those at other missions and a closer look at this period —one of the most important in the history of San Francisco de la Espada—is a portrait of the drama and bloodshed of the mission era.

Apache Indian raids terrorized the missions during 1736 and 1737. Several soldiers and citizens were killed and stock and horses were stolen. Shortly after an attack on a convoy at El Atacoso, the Apaches stole about forty horses from the mission of San Francisco de la Espada. The leader of this band appears to have been "Cabellos Colorados," for the soldiers sent out in pursuit of the raiders captured a worn-out horse, which was recognized as one bought a short time before by an Indian chief from Alférez Juan Galván of San Antonio in exchange for a skin. In 1737 the brutal attack of a band on San Francisco de la Espada is recorded. Five Indian women and two boys from the Mission had gone out to gather fruit on the Medina River. "While there, they were suddenly attacked by a group of Apaches, who killed the five women, horribly desecrated their bodies, slicing their abdomens with fiendish glee, and carried away the two boys." Why the Apaches were on the war path for the period 1736-1737 is disputed. Although there is no proof, it is believed by some that their extreme boldness was based on knowledge many soldiers were deserting from Béxar, weakening the garrison.

Guards on duty at the missions were a deterrent to such attacks and were valuable in other ways. The soldiers were necessary in the mission to maintain order among the naturally frightened neophytes, to help the missionaries perform the daily duties of mission life, and to accompany the padres on their frequent searches for runaway Indians.

On October 8, 1736, Governor Carlos Franquis de Lugo notified Fray Benito de Santa Ana, President of the Querétaran missions in San Antonio, that he had decided to remove two of the three soldiers from each mission. These soldiers, according to the governor, had been assigned to the missions Concepción, San Francisco de la Espada, and San Juan Capistrano by the former Viceroy Marquez de Juan de Acuña Casafuerte, for a period of two years, now long expired. With the desertion of many soldiers the guards from the missions were needed to re-enforce the local garrisons. In attempting to solve his own problem, however, the governor seriously handicapped the progress of the missions. He asked the Father President to notify Fathers Pedro Ysamendi and Joseph Hurtado who were in the other two missions of the order.

With refined irony, the governor, in an attempt to justify his action, declared, "I assure your reverence, in all truth, that I wish I had at my command a sufficiently large garrison to practice the same disregard (of my duty) as my predecessors," broadly hinting the irregularity of the practice. Franquis also removed at the same time two extra guards from the missions of San Antonio de Valero and San José.

To make matters more difficult, the governor informed Fray Benito two days later that he had further decided that Captain Costales of La Bahía should now furnish all the guards, to consist of one man per mission. Costales had earlier supplied soldiers for three of the missions. In addition, since Father Joseph Borruel, of the San José Mission, had informed the governor that he did not really need a guard, Don Gabriel Costales was to send only four men from the garrison at La Bahía, who were to change every month.

With only one soldier or perhaps none to guard them, the Indians found immediate freedom. By April of 1737 they had begun to abandon the missions. More than any other season of the year the neophytes found it hard to remain in the mission in the spring. Soon after Fernández de Jáuregin had become governor in September, he restored three soldiers to each mission in his territory. Unfortunately, the reenforcement arrived too late. In a statement by Father Fray Santa Ana to Captain Joseph (José) de Urrutia of San Antonio on April 12 the missionary said, "You can imagine how the Indians are and what the *Padres* can do when there is not one to incline them to sow the seed and do the chores required for a rational and civilized living."

The missions could not operate without a soldier. Father Santa Ana requested that at least one man be sent to each mission. He also informed Urrutia that the Tacame Indians of the Espada Mission had fled. A missionary had already set out in search of them but an escort of two or three soldiers was needed to assist him. Acting under the orders of Governor Franquis, Captain Urrutia was forced to reply that he could not supply any soldiers to the missions. Urrutia's personal feelings about this letter were stated in a communication to the viceroy on April 18; he felt guilty that he could not assist the missions, but he had to follow his orders.

The flight of the Tacame Indians, beginning in 1736, initiated a long series of mission abandonments. By early summer the mission of San Francisco de la Espada had been abandoned completely. On June 8, 1737, Father Fray Ignacio Ysasmendi, of the Mission San Francisco, went to Father Santa Ana, at the Mission Concepción, to report that his mission had been deserted.

Father Ysasmendi related that a few days preceding the abandonment of San Francisco the neophytes had killed a number of mission cattle without permission and had committed several other offenses. The Father did not punish them, fearing they would do something of greater consequence. He tried to let the incident pass but the result was inevitable.

No one knows the motive behind the desertion. Perhaps the Indians were afraid of being punished. Maybe they were tempted by the knowledge no soldier would restrain them if they decided to abandon the mission. On June 7 the Indians returned to the woods to live.

Until the abandonment, the mission had consisted of 230 Indians, most of which were Christians. "All these souls," exclaimed Father Santa Ana, "have returned to their former barbarous freedom of the wilds." Father Ysasmendi appealed directly to the viceroy for help, but he also took matters into his own hands. He knew that ultimately he could rely on very little assistance from the authorities. Not long after the flight of the Indians Father Ysasmendi had sent a messenger to ask the runaways to return to the mission, giving assurance that they would not be punished. The messenger succeeded in bringing back five adults and two children. The second messenger dispatched by the Father never returned. The third attempt proved to be in vain also.

Father Ysasmendi requested an escort from Governor Prudencio de Orobia y Basterra to accompany him to the woods where the Indians were living. The return of the Indians was vital to the mission. Not only were the crops ready to be harvested, but, more important, many of the Indians were baptized Christians and should not be allowed to continue in their apostasy. The governor complied with the Father's wishes; he sent word to Captain Gabriel Costales at La Bahía to make ten men available for the faithful Padre's needs. Thus, on December 23, Sergeant Miguel Olivares and nine men from La Bahía reported to the governor; and they later accompanied Father Ysasmendi in his search for the Pacao and Arcahomo Indians. The soldiers were instructed to treat the Indians kindly and to assure them that their presence was to protect them against the Apaches. The patience and faith of Father Ysasmendi were rewarded after twenty-one long days of searching for the neophytes in the land of the Pacao and Arcahomo Indians. He succeeded in bringing back 108 of the mission's Indians. According to the records at the mission only twenty-four continued missing, eleven of whom were baptized and thirteen instructed.

An epidemic of smallpox and measles in 1739 were the next impediment to mission progress. The padres were no less zealous in the face of this hardship and worked night and day to bring comfort to the ill, baptize those who were dying, and encourage the faltering. The Indians were well acquainted with this dreaded sickness and believed the only safety was flight. It had been their custom to abandon stricken tribal members. Through exhortation the padres managed to hold some of the Indians at the mission, although many fled. By death or desertion, the losses were great. The affliction drastically cut the numbers. San Francisco de la Espada was reduced from 120 to fifty. Nor did the padres remain unaffected. Many had become ill in their extremely difficult labors. The epidemic was no respecter of race or faiths: Father Fray Ignacio Ysasmendi died during the epidemic, a martyr to charity.

They searched the woods for runaway neophytes. The patience and endurance of the missionaries was undaunted. But at the close of 1740, San Francisco recorded only 121 Indians living within its mission.

Urrutia's report to the viceroy gave a detailed account of the work of the missionaries in the San Antonio missions describing the devotion typified by the San Francisco priests. He told that the padres were working untiringly to provide the Indians with both spiritual and worldly assistance. Not only were the neophytes instructed twice a day in the *doctrina*, but they also learned how to plant and harvest crops. The padres realized after long, bitter experience, that new Indians brought into the missions could not be expected to perform as those previously in residence. Therefore, new entries were gradually introduced into the system of work and discipline, so foreign to the savage nature of Indians. Urrutia continued his report to the viceroy by pointing out that frequently the 450 *pesos* given to each missionary for personal needs was used to supplement the comfort and welfare of the neophytes. There was also a medicine chest and a missionary who administered to the sick. In short, Urrutia's account of the missions was favorable towards the work and devotion which the padres had provided.

There was a period from 1740 to 1780 which was perhaps the mission's most stable and prosperous time. It had survived the Apache raids, removal of soldiers, Indian abandonments and epidemics, all during the early stages of its establishment. In 1745, Father Ortiz made a visit to San Francisco at which time he noted that since the mission's removal from East Texas to San Antonio in 1731, 393 Indians had been baptized, 213 had received the last sacraments and had been given Christian burial, and that there were 204 persons of both sexes and all ages living in the mission. Of these, 180 were baptized Christians and twenty-four were being instructed.

Father Ortiz reported in 1745 that the pueblo consisted mainly of *jacales*, huts made of brush, mud, and straw, grouped about the church. The missionaries lived in a two-story house of stone and mortar, with two cells on the second floor and two downstairs, used as offices. On the farm outside the mission walls the Indians planted five *fanegas* of corn and raised about a thousand; two *fanegas* of beans which yielded about forty; and several patches of melons and pumpkins which kept the natives well supplied, and a field of cotton.

Little specific information about life at the Mission San Francisco de la Espada is known until the 1780's. Fray Juan Augustín Morfi, noted Franciscan Missionary, teacher, and historian, on an inspection tour of Texas in 1777-1778, recorded the following specific facts about San Francisco de la Espada:

> SAN FRANCISCO DE LA ESPADA. One quarter of a league from the preceding mission and three from the presidio of San Antonio, on the west side of the river, is the mission of Nuestro Santo Padre San Francisco de la Espada, companion mission of Concepción and San Juan Capistrano in point of origin, and like them removed at the same time (to its present site). The church was demolished because it threatened to fall down, and services are being held in an ample room that has a choir and a sacristy, all very neat. The convent is laid out on a straight line, with four cells on the second floor and three on the first, galleries, workshop, and a good-sized granary, all made of stone, but ill-arranged and plain. The pueblo or Indian quarters consist of three rows of houses that form a square with the convent, a wall, likewise of stone, closing a portion of the enclosure where there are no houses. It was founded for the Pacaos, Borrados, and Mariquitas. From the time of its establishment to the year 1761, there were 815 persons baptized and 513 buried. Today there are 40 families with 133 persons.
>
> Between the presidio, villa, and the five missions described they make up 514 families: 759 men, 613 women, 373 boys, 300 girls, 4 male slaves, and 11 female slaves, totaling in all 2060 persons, of whom 324 are Spanish, or as they commonly say "de razon" [literally sensible"], 268 Indians, 16 mestizos, and 151 "de color quebrado" [literally "of broken color," meaning colored].

It was about this period in the history of the San Antonio missions that a drastic change was contemplated by the Spanish officials. The missions in the northern Interior Provinces of Coahuila, Nuevo Santander, and Texas had been a constant drain on the royal treasury. The usual practice, according to that which was observed in the more populated regions of Mexico and as set forth in the general provisions of the Laws of the Indies, was to maintain the mission for a ten year period, after which it was turned over to the neophytes. The surplus products or wealth was distributed among the neophytes; the ordinary took control of the priests' quarters, ornaments, vestments, sacred vessels, and other property. In short the Mission disappeared and a new, self-supporting community grew up. Much to the displeasure of the Spanish officials, the ten years had been extended to more than half a century in the case of the Texas missions.

The process of secularization of the Texas missions was hindered for various reasons, beyond the understanding of the authorities in Spain and Mexico. The Texas missions existed throughout the first half century in a primitive stage, unable to elevate their position because of particular regional problems. The Indians with whom the missionaries in Texas worked were extremely nomadic and barbaric by nature. The primitive civilization of the Indians and the presence of European rivals—the French traders in particular—doubly complicated the task of the missionaries.

The actual secularization was brought about inadvertently and as a matter of financial expediency. In an attempt to spread the faith and reach new tribes, a follower of the College of Zacatecas promoted the secularization of Valero and the reduction of the other four missions in San Antonio to two. Father Fray Manuel Silva, newly elected commissary and prefect of the missions of the College of Zacatecas, visited Texas in 1790. While inspecting the existing missions he conceived a plan to reach and convert the wild coastal tribes. Fray Silva proposed the establishment of a new mission in the Presidio of La Bahía along with similar missions to be located from the mouth of the Colorado to the villages of the Taovayas.

In 1792, Father Silva returned to Mexico to present the details of his plan to the viceroy. The new missions, with adequate military guards, would be located for contact with the tribes along the entire Gulf coast. Moreover, it was hoped that eventually the tribes living along the rivers which flowed into the Gulf would be "brought into the faith." The ultimate goal of the missions was to extend their work to the Comanches. Father Silva knew his plan would never be accepted if additional money had to be drawn from the royal treasury. His proposal was as follows: The existing mission of Valero would be secularized, the four San Antonio missions would consolidate into two, and the two missionaries assigned to the new settlement at Nacogdoches would be released. In this manner various missionaries would be available, with no added expense to the royal treasury, to establish missions in the coastal area.

Orders were issued in January, 1793, that the mission Valero be secularized and the four San Antonio missions reorganize into two. The proposal for the change at Nacogdoches was refused. Although originally only Valero was to be secularized, the inevitable result was that all of the missions of San Antonio were.

Governor Manuel Muñoz believed secularization of the missions must transpire gradually. On June 25, 1794, Muñoz wrote to the commandant general advising that the process would be effected as circumstances permitted. The missions, at that time, were in such a precarious position that secularization was almost impossible. San Francisco de la Espada had only fifteen Indians, most of whom were sick or aged. The holdings were meager: Espada had eight yoke of oxen, one cow, five horses, about 1,300 sheep, and six bushels of corn planted. Another factor in secularization was the impending crop harvest and the need of resulting money to pay off debts which the missions owed for supplies.

Although the governor was pleading for time in the secularization process, he complied with his orders by requesting that inventories be made at each mission. July 11 was set as the date for secularization which would begin with San Francisco de la Espada. On this date in 1794, Governor Muñoz went to the San Francisco mission where he was met by Father Fray Pedro Noreña, minister in charge, and by José Lázaro de los Santos, the newly appointed *justicia*. At this time the mission Indians were called together and the decree of the commandant general read and explained to them. There were only fifteen neophytes, three of whom were old and disabled. According to the terms of the decree the Indians were to share the mission property, administer and increase it.

The following day the actual survey and distribution of the land took place. Eight plats, four hundred by two hundred *varas* each, were first surveyed and set aside as communal lands of the mission pueblo. Fifteen other plats were surveyed, each three hundred by two hundred *varas*, one of which was assigned to each Indian in the San Francisco mission. Any lands which they could not cultivate should be rented to the Spaniards with the consent of *Justicia* José Lazaro de los Santos. Furthermore, the woods and pasture lands of the mission now belonged to the neophytes and they could demand rent from any person who used them for his private stock and cattle.

In addition to the distribution of land the Indians were given, on the same day, eight yoke of oxen fully equipped, eleven plows, nine harrows, and four hoes with handles; twenty-five pounds of iron, three pounds of steel; three crowbars, five axes, one bucksaw, a handsaw, an English saw, a compass, four bits, a pair of beam scales, a brass scale, a small brass frame; two one-pound cannons weighing 256 pounds, and ninety-eight pounds of lead; fifteen pairs of shears, 875 pounds of wool, and two looms complete with their respective combs, cards, spinning wheels, and shuttles; a mare and three horses, three mules, and nine sets of harness, a cow with a calf, and 1,150 head of sheep.

The Indians did not receive the sheep and lambs. They were left to the care of Joaquín Lerma who agreed to lend them. Lerma was to be given eight *pesos*, two bushels of corn, and a *peso* and a half of cigarettes each month for his services. He was not to receive payment until after the sheep had been sheared.

After the distribution, Governor Muñoz reviewed for the neophytes the method to be observed in the administration of their individual property, the cultivation of their lands, and the disposal of the crops raised. The plot of land called "jardín," surveyed for the secular priest, was to be cultivated at his own expense.

A follow-up survey report was made in June, 1809, by the governor on the San Antonio missions. (It should be remembered that when the missions were secularized, there were a number of neophytes still under instruction and that the two missions at La Bahía were exempted from the secularization decree.) The governor noted that in the San Francisco mission there were fourteen men and ten women. Besides Indians numerous Spaniards had been attracted to the missions where they had rented land and lived. San Francisco listed fifty-one men and forty-two women. Every Indian had a house within the walls of the mission and had been assigned a *Suerte* for cultivation. The Indians should have been given the title to the lands assigned to them, but, unfortunately, the officials had neglected to carry out this part of the instructions.

Governor Mañuel de Salcedo (1810-1813) made a description of the boundaries of each of the missions. The boundaries given for San Francisco were quite vague. They ran from the back of the mission north to a small dam on the river and west from this point to the ranch of Luis Pérez. Its lands were bounded on the east by the Delgado property, and on the south by Atascoso Creek. Although the property was administered by the Indian governor and a *padre*, neither was capable of managing them properly. The productivity of the land was poor. Moreover, the missions, in general, had become a haven for idlers and gamblers; the churches were in fair condition.

The period from 1813 to 1818 was characterized by foreign intrigues and turmoil. The struggle for independence from Spain kept the land in constant chaos.

Throughout all the fighting, records were maintained on the missions. These records, however, were almost totally destroyed during the devastating Gutiérrez-Magee invasion, a filibustering expedition of 1812-1813. Consequently, Father Vallejo was not able to prepare a detailed report on a comparative basis.

A report by Father Vallejo, dated February 11, 1815, listed mission Espada with twenty-seven Indians and seventy-two Spaniards. Whether they resided at the mission or not, they received instructions in the Christian doctrine every Sunday. The principal occupation of the natives at all of the missions was cultivating corn. Although some of the fields were irrigated and produced good harvests, others were dependent on the rainfall which determined the size of the crop. Unfortunately, since 1794, when the San Antonio missions were secularized, they had no common capital. By this time, Father Vallejo observed that the natives were practically destitute for they did not know how to manage the land which was given to them. Religious services were not the responsibility of the Indians but were provided for by an annual stipend of 450 pesos which were given to the minister by the royal treasury. The chapels were in a fair state of preservation and well provided with all the necessary images and vestments for services.

Destruction was the keynote of this period of Texas history, even extending into the 1830's. The mission system had been secularized in the previous century, and the missions since then had lost their vital force. The fact the missionaries never lost their zeal and faith underscores their unselfish love for the Indians of Texas.

Most of the mission lands had been disposed of in 1794; the priests' quarters, the mission buildings, and the stone in the massive walls remained as property of the mission. After many conflicting orders a final decision to sell all mission property at a public auction was made. Thus in September of 1831, Governor José

María Letona wrote Músquiz that all property would be sold except the chapels, which were to continue to be used as churches. The money received from the public auction was to be deposited and held by the city treasurer until further notice.

While government officials were involved in disputes over the distribution and auction of the mission land, the missions themselves were still involved in various conflicts. Through appeals to the Commandant, Mateo Ahumada, troops were to be sent to the missions to afford protection from hostile Indians. Continuing Indian attacks were hindering the mission Indians and settlers from planting and harvesting their crops. In the spring of 1826 a band of Comanches attacked the Mission of San Francisco and stole the green corn, killed the stock, and wounded several men. Following the arrival of the soldiers at the mission, however, the attacks subsided for the remainder of that year. A census taken in 1829 showed twenty-eight people living at Mission San Francisco.

The plaza and its defenses at Espada have suffered destructive forces of man and nature and shared in important Texas history. It was here that the Texas Army, led by James Bowie and James W. Fannin, Jr., reported the capture of the mission on October 22, 1835, and Ammon Underwood recorded on October 25th that "About 100 Americans who had taken possession of the Mission Espada were attacked by a body of about 200 Mexicans but the Mexicans soon retreated."

Another significant mention of Espada Mission was made by George Wilkins Kendall who was in San Antonio in 1841 before leaving on the Texan Santa Fé Expedition. Kendall wrote in his *Narrative of the Texan Santa Fe Expedition* that although La Espada was inhabited, "the church, however, is in ruins. Two sides of the square consist of mere walls; the other sides are composed of dwellings. . . ."

The history of the mission of San Francisco de la Espada would not be complete without the story of a man who did so much to continue and preserve its tradition. Father Francis Bouchu, born in France in 1829, came to America in 1855 where he was a lawyer, teacher, photographer, mechanic, printer, and historian, with a great deal of knowledge about missions themselves. For almost fifty years, 1858 to 1907, Father Bouchu served as the missionary at San Francisco. During his years at the mission he administered faithfully to the spiritual wants of the Mexicans in the vicinity, holding services in the chapel which he himself had rebuilt. Education of the children was also provided by Father Bouchu. He conducted a Sunday school class in Spanish. There was no adequate textbook which these simple folk could understand; so, he wrote one himself and printed four editions on his own press. Father Bouchu was a little eccentric—he would rarely be photographed, his reason being that he didn't want anyone to laugh at his picture. He liked living alone and, even when he became feeble in old age, he refused to have anyone wait upon him. It eventually became necessary to remove Father Bouchu to Santa Rosa Infirmary, where he died at the age of seventy-eight.

The Mission of San Francisco is indebted to Father Bouchu not only for the spiritual guidance which he gave but also for the manual labor which he provided. The good state of repair of the chapel at San Francisco is a result of the untiring efforts of the Father. Upon his arrival at the mission, only the front and rear walls were standing. With his own hands he built up the side walls on their old foundations, plastered and whitewashed them, put in a wooden floor, hung doors on the entrances, and covered the chapel with a tin roof. He made a chancel railing, a choir loft, and benches to furnish the interior of the chapel. The altar once again had the necessary ornaments, with the original statues re-gilded of Saint Francis, the Blessed Virgin, and Christ Crucified. Since then, several restorations have been made in 1883 and 1911.

The structures remaining today are few: the chapel

is in reasonably good repair, as is the aqueduct outside the mission walls, one fortified tower on the southeast corner of the plaza, and a few ruins of the stone houses in which the Indians lived. The room adjoining the fort is now used as a display room.

Since 1922, the care of San Francisco de la Espada has been invested in the Redemptorist Fathers, an order founded on November 9, 1732, by Saint Adolphus de Liguori, which has as its purpose the conduct of missions and retreats. In 1915 the Sisters of the Incarnate Word began a school at the mission which has continued until today.

A beautiful tribute to the original founders has been paid by Zephyrin Engelhardt, author of several works dealing with Franciscan missionaries and missions, who has written that, "The Franciscan friars came as messengers of Christ. Their message was the Gospel as preached by Christ and His Apostles. Like the Apostles they had severed every tie that interfered with the delivery of this message. They had given up relatives, friends, property, prospects, and mother-country for the sake of attracting souls to Christ." The great faith and strength of these dedicated men permeates Espada Mission and grounds today, and reaches out to command the respect and admiration of the visitor to this historic mission.

San Jose

Mission San Jose

San Jose

by

James M. Day

Not far from San Antonio
    Stands the church of San José
Brightly its walls are gilded
    With the sun's departing ray
The long grass twines the arches through,
    And, stirred by evening air,
Wave gracefully the vine's dark leaves,
    And bends the prickly pear.

Mission San José has stood the test of time and history to become known as the "Queen" of Texas missions. In its time it was prosperous and successful, serving well the purposes for which it was founded. Architecturally functional and beautiful, San José successfully blended Spanish architecture and building methods with the construction materials of a raw frontier. It survives to serve as an instructional shrine for all who will come and look and learn of the Spanish heritage of Texas.

The story of San José begins in 1519 when the efficient but ruthless Spaniard, Hernando Cortés, invaded and conquered the Aztec Empire. His success opened the door of conquest for Spain in North America. Soon other Castilian *capitanos* were exploring and conquering the southern and central regions of Mexico. By the late 1500's and early 1600's the tentacles of Spanish conquest were edging across and up the Rio Grande, and by the late 1600's its influence had reached along the Pacific coast in California.

In expanding her colonial holdings, Spain used the accepted imperialistic formula: conquering, converting, controlling and then exploiting the natives. To make this policy as effective and efficient as possible, special institutions were formed for each purpose. For conquest, it was the *conquistador*, a campaigning general backed by an army. For conversion it was the friar, or padre, who was characteristically on the extreme edge of the frontier, converting the Indians to Christianity.

In the beginning of the Spanish occupation of Mexico, the soldier led the conquest and penetration into the vast interior, but in northern Mexico and in Texas, the friar took the lead, and the soldiers had to follow to protect him and his converts. After the conquest was completed, the *encomienda*, or economic system, was placed into operation to exploit the wealth of the area and the labor of the natives. The *conquistador* became an *encomendero*. In northern Mexico the *encomienda* eventually came to be known as the *hacienda*, and when smaller areas of land were involved, the *rancho*. Soon too, missions were established so that the padres could centralize and formalize their conversion efforts. These were the men and the institutions that Spain used to expand her frontiers, and they were fairly successful until they reached the arid area of Texas and into the lair of the cunning Apache and the cruel Comanche.

From 1685 (when the enterprising Frenchman, Robert Cavelier, Sieur de La Salle, established Fort St. Louis on Matagorda Bay) to 1763 (when the Treaty of Paris was signed ending the Seven Years War), Spain and France were rivals on the Texas scene. The presence of the French served as a spur in the side of the Spanish officials in the new world, goading them into action and further conquest. La Salle's intrusion proved temporary, but the Spaniards reacted to it by establishing missions in East Texas and exploring the other regions north of the Rio Grande. When France again threatened East Texas early in the eighteenth century, Spain once again was spurred into action. In 1716 Captain Domingo Ramón led an expedition into Texas to create permanent settlements. He was accompanied by two missionaries, Father Fray Felix Isidro de Espinosa of the College of Querétaro and Father Fray Antonio Margil de Jesús of the College of Zacatecas. This was the first time that the Zacatecas (a relatively new college) had entered the mission field in Texas. The two priests labored in the East Texas missions until 1719, when war broke out between France and Spain, forcing the Spaniards to abandon the missions in the east. San Antonio became the point of retreat. Padre Espinosa, however, elected to go farther, to Monclova and then on to Mexico City. Padre Margil, on the other hand, remained at San Antonio and there, in the following year, founded what was considered to have been the most successful mission in Texas—San José y San Miguel de Aguayo.

The most beautiful and most prosperous of all Texas missions—and one of the finest in all North America—had its taproot, as did all missions in Texas, in Mexico, where the Spanish mission system was first developed and where it flourished. The purpose of the mission as visualized by the government of New Spain was threefold: first, to Christianize the Indian; second, to teach him the habits and customs of Western civilization and thus make him an effective, self-sustaining subject of the king; and third, to extend the authority of the Spanish crown and hold the land against all intruders.

The mission itself belonged to both the church and the state. Actually the missionary was an employee, a sort of good will ambassador, of the king. Although the padres were selected by the missionary colleges or seminaries, their remuneration (usually 450 pesos per year) was doled out of the royal treasury; and their appointment as missionaries had to have the viceroy's approval. Inasmuch as all of the padre's needs were taken care of by the church, the stipend granted him was used by the college to maintain the mission. New missions could not be founded without the consent of the viceroy, and both the church and the state shared the undertaking. The government bore the initial expense of building and furnishing the mission, and the evangelical college was charged with maintaining it.

The missionaries who served in Texas belonged to the notable Franciscan order, and all but a few of them were sent either by the College of Santa Cruz de Querétaro (established in 1683) or by the College of Nuestra de Guadalupe de Zacatecas (established in 1707). Mission San José y San Miguel de Aguayo was established by and for the Zacatecan brotherhood.

The year is 1720; the place is San Antonio; the man is Fray Antonio Margil de Jesús—one of the unsung heroes of Spanish Texas. What manner of man was this tireless, dedicated, fearless priest? Father Margil was born in Valencia, Spain, on August 18, 1657, and dedicated his life to the church at an early age. At fifteen, he knocked on the massive oak doors of the Franciscan Convent of La Corona de Cristo in Valencia and sought admission to the Order of Friars Minor, commonly known as Franciscans. His request for admittance was granted, Margil took the religious vows of poverty, chastity, and obedience. When he was twenty-four years of age (in 1671) he was ordained a priest and thus realized the first of his many goals in life. Soon after being ordained, he became confessor and preacher in the town of Onda, Spain; but he moved on, a few years later, to the picturesque Mediterranean port of Denia.

In 1683, seeking a greater challenge, Father Margil joined a group of missionaries preparing to sail for New Spain. He landed at Vera Cruz on June 6, and immediately became associated with the Missionary College of Santa Cruz de Querétaro. From this center, the indomitable priest traveled far and wide throughout Central America and Mexico, seeking converts for the church. His quest for Christian converts carried him to Yucatan, Costa Rica, Nicaragua, and Guatemala. On January 12, 1707, Father Margil founded the College of Guadalupe in Zacatecas.

Father Zephyrin Englehardt, O.F.M., dean of historians writing on the missions in the United States, says of this Apostle to the Indians:

> He always walked barefooted, without sandals, fasted every day in the year, never used meat or fish, and applied discipline (scourage) as well as other instruments of penance to himself unmercifully. He slept very little, but passed in prayer the greater part of the night as well as the time allotted for the siesta. The result was that his efforts for the salvation of Indians and colonists were crowned with extraordinary success.

As previously stated, Father Margil accompanied the Ramón Expedition to East Texas in 1716. Here he was instrumental in founding the Missions of Guadalupe, Dolores, and San Miguel among different tribes of Indians. In 1719 Father Margil retreated with the Spanish frontier to San Antonio, where he founded San José, the queen of the missions, in 1720. In mid-1721, after a short period of time in East Texas, where he labored to rebuild the missions destroyed by the French, Margil returned to San Antonio and the Mission San José,

> where he continued to work for the spiritual good of the Indians; and where he continued to till the soil, alone, and with scanty food, which consisted regularly of a little cooked corn, seasoned with bear grease, and natural salt of the earth when that was found. A bit of chocolate or the black meat of a crow was a great delicacy for the reverend father. His bed consisted of a small spread of black wool, upon the ground, with the gloomy and hard trunk of a tree for his pillow.

During this second short period at San Jose, Father Margil compiled a work of infinite value—a dictionary of the various and intricate Indian dialects. Thus he was able to assist those padres who came after him.

In 1722 this pioneer priest of the Texas prairies returned to Mexico to take up his appointment as Guardian of the College of Guadalupe in Zacatecas. After his term of office expired, Fray Margil again took up missionary work, this time in western Mexico. He died in the famous Convento de San Francisco, August 6, 1726; his last words were: "My heart is ready, O God, my heart is ready." In 1861, the mortal remains of the humble priest, who wanted to be known only as "la misma nada" ("the same nobody"), were removed to the Cathedral of Mexico. The beautiful mission of San José on the San Antonio River is a just monument to this devoted, dedicated, and determined missionary priest.

The desire to Christianize the heathen members of the Coahuiltecan tribes became one of the driving motives of Padre Margil's life. Although sixty-two years of age when he was at San Antonio in 1719, the good father began to administer to the Pampopas, the Pastías, and the Suliajames Indians who lived along the San Antonio River several leagues south of the original mission at San Antonio, San Antonio de Valero (Alamo).

As he worked with the natives, the idea came to him that the Zacatecans should have a mission at San Antonio to Christianize the Indians as the Querétarans were doing at San Antonio de Valero under Padre Antonio de San Buenaventura Olivares. Margil's idea was converted to action when on the day after Christmas, 1719, he took pen in hand and wrote a detailed, dramatic, and persuasive letter to the new governor and captain-general of the Provinces of Coahuila and Texas, the Marquis de Aguayo.

Don Joseph de Azlor Y Virto de Vera, the second Marquis of San Miguel de Aguayo, came from an old Spanish family which had rendered valorous military and long civilian service to the kings of Aragon. By virtue of his marriage to Marchioness Ignacia Xaviera, the twice widowed daughter of Don Agustín de Echevers, first Marquis of San Miguel de Aguayo, Don Joseph became the second Marquis. He and his wife moved to New Spain in 1712 and settled in Coahuila. When the Ramón Expedition was being provisioned in 1716, the Marquis de Aguayo donated two hundred head of cattle to the cause. At this time the Marquis probably had the occasion to know Padre Margil. When the French again threatened Spanish Texas in 1719, the Marquis de Aguayo offered "his fortune, his life, and his sword" to the service of the king. No doubt this outburst of dramatic patriotism was instrumental in his being appointed Governor of Coahuila and Texas by the Viceroy of New Spain, the Marquis de Valero. The Marquis de Aguayo was preparing for an orientation trip to Texas when he received Padre Margil's dispatch of December 26, 1719.

In the letter Padre Margil congratulated the Marquis on his new appointment before getting to the real purpose of his writing. He stated that the friars of Querétero and Zacatecas were working in perfect harmony in Christianizing the Indians, that each group had established three missions in East Texas, and that all had been forced to return to the San Antonio River valley, where only the Queréterans had a mission, San Antonio de Valero. This mission was doing good work. Seeing the splendid crop of corn raised by the mission Indians caused other Indians in the area to want to live in pueblos under the care of missionaries. Father Margil painted the San Antonio River valley in glowing terms, expressing the belief that the region was "destined to be the heart" of the effort in founding missions —the Queréterans going northward to New Mexico and the Zacatecans going south to Tampico. But the Zacatecans needed a mission of their own at San Antonio, a request that brought Padre Margil to the point of his letter.

Margil suggested that a Zacatecan mission be founded immediately and named Mission de San José y San Miguel de Aguayo in honor of the governor—a shrewd piece of psychology and salesmanship on the part of Padre Margil. All that the Marquis de Aguayo had to do was to issue orders to Captain Juan Valdéz at San Antonio to select a suitable site and then give possession of the area to Padre Margil. A statue of Saint Joseph was already available as was the other church property necessary for the celebration of Mass and the administration of the Sacraments. These items, he wrote the Marquis, he had brought from the abandoned missions of East Texas. Indians were in the area, eager to be Christianized and willing to be loyal subjects of the king; and he had beads, trinkets, and clothes to attract them. All that was needed was the permission of his excellency, the Governor of Coahuila and Texas.

Flattered, of course, to have a mission named in his honor, Aguayo responded quickly. In a letter to Captain Valdéz, dated January 22, 1720, the governor instructed the commander of the Spanish forces at San Antonio to select a site for a second mission and turn it over to Padre Margil. Apparently competition for Christian converts was keen between the two colleges, for when Padre Olivares of Valero Mission learned of the Governor's decision, he determined to see Valdéz register a strong protest. On February 23, 1720, Olivares, accompanied by the officers and Indians of San Antonio de Valero, appeared before Captain Valdéz to complain against the proposed new mission on the grounds that the Queréterans had exclusive conversion and mission rights at San Antonio. He also informed the captain that the Indians he had converted and the ones that Margil was proposing to evangelize were traditional enemies and that serious trouble would result from their being so close together. Valdéz, who took his orders from the governor, listened patiently to the complaint of the Queréterans but informed them that he could do nothing about the decision. He had to comply with the Marquis de Aguayo's wishes.

The next day Valdéz summoned Padre Olivares and Padre Margil, the neophytes (converts) of San Antonio de Valero, members of the Pampopa, Suliajame, and Pastía nations, and approximately eighty soldiers to accompany him down the San Antonio River to select a site for the new mission. Padre Olivares, pleading illness, asked to be excused from what promised to be a victory expedition for the College of Zacatecas. (Padre Joseph Guerra officially represented the College of Querétero and the "ailing" Olivares). A site a little over three leagues from San Antonio de Valero was selected where there was a large plain that would lend itself to irrigation. Valdéz dedicated the area chosen "for the service of God," designated the general positions of the pueblo, the church, the cemetery, the hospital, the jail, and the public square, and ordered the immediate election of officers. Juan, Chief of the Pampopas, became governor; Nicolas of the Suliajames was made *alcalde* (mayor or judge); and Alonzo, Chief of the Pastías, was elected *alquacil* (sheriff). *Regidores* (commissioners) were Francisco, a Pampopa, and Antonio, a Suliajame.

After the selection of the site, its official dedication, and the election of officers, Captain Valdéz and the representatives of the Mission San Antonio de Valero departed. The Indians, the minor government officials that remained, and the missionaries of Zacatecas then proceeded to carry out the customary informal mission dedication ceremonies. They first went to the point on the San Antonio River where the water for irrigation was to be taken out. The spot was blessed. From there the group walked over the land allotted to the mission, examining the texture of the soil, the pasture land, the woods, and the general lay of the land. A high spot, about three leagues (7½ miles) from the Mission of San Antonio de Valero was finally selected as the site for the main building of the new mission. The missionaries and officials then shook hands with the Indian chiefs, and by means of an interpreter explained their duties to them. They were told that it would be "their duty to till the soil, to receive instruction in the Christian faith, to send their children to the mission school, and to learn to worship the Lord and keep His commandments." Then in a final act consummating the dedication "weeds were pulled up, stones thrown about, handfuls of dust scattered in the wind, and branches of trees cut in sign of possession." Exact locations were then designated for the Indian pueblo, the church, the cemetery, the monastery, the hospital, and the barracks for the guards. Thus began Mission San José.

Three groups of people were involved in building San José—the priests, the Indians, and the soldiers. The padres taught Christianity as well as the methods of farming and the trades. The Indians were the subjects who learned and performed the labor. Once they were converted and became neophytes they administered the government, subject to supervision by the padres. To see that the mission functioned without violence, from within or without, soldiers were sent from the *presidio* (fort) located a mile and a half upstream. The soldiers were probably needed for a time, at least until the Indians became accustomed to mission life with its strict discipline and long hours of labor. After a few years the Spanish troops were no longer needed and trusted neophytes were assigned to serve as guards and soldiers. When Governor Don Carlos Franquis de Lugo (successor to Marquis de Aguayo) announced in October, 1736, that the soldiers were needed elsewhere and would be withdrawn, Padre Joseph Borruel of San José offered no objection.

The years passed, and San José grew steadily and developed into a compact self-supporting community. As in all missions, the first buildings at San José were constructed of adobe. These hard earthen houses and buildings were soon replaced by stone structures, crops were abundant, converts were many and the mission San José prospered. By the middle 1730's the mission had become known as one of the most successful in Texas. The two missionaries who labored here after Father Margil returned to Mexico in 1722, and who must be given credit for developing the mission complex on a permanent basis were first, Father Miguel Nuñez and then, Father Agustín Patrón.

This area of progressive development was suddenly arrested when tragedy struck the mission early in 1739. An epidemic of measles and smallpox swept through San José and the surrounding area. The epidemic was of such magnitude that it set the development and progress of San José back at least a decade. Losses by death and desertion numbered in the hundreds. The epidemic jeopardized the entire mission system in the San Antonio area. The padres at San José labored long and hard to save lives, to comfort the sick, to baptize those who were close to death, and to persuade those who were healthy to remain at their posts. This last task was the most difficult of all, for one of the old beliefs of the Indians was to abandon those who had the dreadful disease. Even though they had been converted, many of the Indians held on to some of their old customs and prejudices—hence, many fled the mission trying to elude the icy fingers of the grim reaper. Burials were made at night in an attempt to hide from the Indians the number of those dying. Prior to the epidemic the mission contained well over three hundred inhabitants, by late 1739 fewer than fifty remained. For months the spectre of death hovered over the queen of the missions, crops were unattended, livestock wandered away and buildings fell into disrepair. By the summer of 1740 the worst had passed, and those who had survived took up the task of rebuilding and regathering and, in some cases, reconverting. In the late months of 1740 the population of San José had climbed to 249—the storm had been weathered.

After the terrible epidemic San José was slowly rebuilt, and by mid-century had again become the glory of the Texas missions. For much of this early period and even as late as the 1790's the archives are missing; hence few facts are available about the building process and those who performed the tasks. Occasionally an inspector or visitor came to the mission and reported his observations. From such reports came the only detailed information available for this valuable period of San José's history.

The Zacatecans at San José did not actively publicize their work. They had failed even to keep the Spanish officials apprised of what they were doing. Therefore, when they requested an augmentation to their staff in 1748, the Council of the Indies refused. This refusal to send additional priests was made in the belief that the Zacatecans were accomplishing little if anything for the glory of God or the Crown. Finally, in October, 1749, a report on the mission was requested by the Council of the Indies from Father Ignacio Antonio Ciprián, the Guardian of the College of Zacatecas. Father Ciprián's report was very flattering. He gave a brief history of Mission San José before declaring that it was the mission that had progressed the most spiritually and temporally and that it had been built so strong that it was a "veritable fortress." As a matter of fact, Padre Ciprián remarked that the feared Apaches would not hesitate to attack the *presidio* at San Antonio, but refrained from attacking San José. However, several of the Indians working in the fields had fallen victim to the Apache rascals, the same tribe that was to give the United States cavalry such a trying time a century and a quarter later.

The Guardian of the College of Zacatecas observed that the mission had a friary of stone with arched corridors, and a church capable of "accommodating 200 persons." Speaking of the progress made by the neophytes at San José Father Ciprián explains:

> They not only comply with the duties of the Church but many of them frequent the sacraments during the year. On Saturday they say the rosary outdoors and sing it very sweetly and with much devotion. They are all dressed in cotton and woolen cloth from the mission where they weave it themselves in their modest looms. They have two thousand head of cattle and one thousand sheep. Of corn they harvest fifteen hundred *fanegas* (three thousand bushels) each year, and if they planted more, they could raise more. When the Indians in this mission are administered the sacrament of Baptism, they resign their practice of polygamy and after they choose one wife, they are duly married by the church.

A decade passed before another glimpse of San José was recorded for history. The observer this time was Jacinto Barrios y Jáuregia, governor of the state of Coahuila and Texas—a man not particularly friendly to the missions but a keen and fair observer. Governor Barrios visited the mission in 1758, and at that time he noted that San José had 281 Indians, of which 113 were men capable of bearing arms, 76 were women, 48 were boys and 44 were girls of various ages—all were Christians. Barrios recognized that San José had reached an "enviable stage of development" and that it was "the best organized and best defended of the five missions (de Valero, San José, Concepción, San Juan, and Espada) in San Antonio." In its existence of thirty-eight years the church's representatives had baptized 964 neophytes, had administered Christian burials to 466, and had performed 145 marriages.

Barrios reported that much credit for the success of the mission had to be given to Father Fray Ildefonso José Marmolejo, who was quite accomplished at "converting the natives from wild heathens to civilized Christians." The government of the missions had been turned over completely to the Indians, who selected their own governor, *cabildo* (governing council), *alcaldes* (judges), *fiscales* (overseers), captains, and lesser officers who managed all military affairs. Anyone who failed to attend prayer or do his assigned task was tried and sentenced by Indian officials. The system apparently was successful, for the Governor remarked that the mission had no jail; there were no fugitives, and there were no Indians in chains or stocks. Barrios further observed that the neophytes were well clothed, had an ample supply of food, worked willingly, and appeared "happy and contented."

Governor Barrios provided an interesting and valuable narrative on the physical plant of the Mission San José de Aguayo as it existed in 1758.

This Mission has 84 apartments [houses] built of stone all in line according to plan, with flat roofs, parapets, and loopholes. These are divided into four squares. Each apartment consists of a room and a kitchen, with its *metate* [stone to grind corn], a pot, a *comal* [flat piece of iron to cook corn cakes], a water jar, closet, pantry, bed, and dresser. Each square has a swimming pool. Four tiers of eighteen apartments or houses each make a square with a cloistered patio where there are ovens and flowing water for the accommodation of Indian women. In like manner the soldier's quarters have a swimming pool, opposite the church. In the space between is found the cemetery, which is more than eighty varas square, surrounded by a wall made of wood with three entrances. It serves as a *plaza* or military square where the natives have their rifle practice and their military exercises not like those of our troops, but their diligence and obedience to commands is admirable. There are four other squares formed by the soldiers' quarters, the carpentry shop, the barn, and the work shop, besides the offices, the sugar mill [the first in Texas] where they make *piloncillo* [brown sugar bars], and cane syrup. There is also a convent and a church. Every thing is arranged with such perfect symmetry that it provokes the admiration of all those who see it. . . . The Mission has a church with one nave and its transept, capable of seating two thousand persons. It has its tower, well proportioned, with its set of bells. The ornaments are of good quality and the images, all in relief, are beautiful.

Barrios noted that the fields, which were all irrigated, grew corn, beans, and sugar cane. Thirty yoke of oxen and the necessary plowing and hoeing implements were on hand to help plant and harvest the bountiful crops. In the granary were 5,000 bushels of corn. In the corral were 1,500 head of cattle (all branded),— the herd, he was told, had been considerably larger but the Apaches had killed over 2,000 head the past few years. The mission had 3,376 head of sheep (by actual count), 103 horses for the use of the herders, 80 mares, and numerous chickens. Beef was the staple meat and seven beeves were killed each week to provide food— four for the mission, one for the *pastores* (sheep herders), one for the cowhands, and one was used to make jerked beef. When a neophyte became sick, he was given chicken broth and lamb chops, a diet not inconsistent with present-day infirmary practices. The evidence presented by Governor Barrios makes a good case for the accomplishments of San José and the mission system; however, its full potential was yet to be reached.

Fray Simón de Hierro, Guardian of the College of Guadalupe, visited San José in 1762. He noted about the same things that Governor Barrios had reported four years earlier but did make one new observation; the Indians were raising all the cotton that went into their clothes. Thus Texas was introduced early to the great staple crop that would provide the backbone for her rural economy after the Civil War.

Probably the most astute observer to visit San José during the eighteenth century was Fray Gaspar José de Solís, inspector of missions for the College of Zacatecas. Inspector Solís paid the mission a three-week visit in the spring of 1768, a decade after Governor Barrios had been there. He looked into every facet of the mission's operation and made a comprehensive report to the College. He seems to have been tremendously impressed with what he saw; and his observations, no doubt, have much to do with the fact that Mission San José de Aguayo was generally regarded as the most beautiful, the most efficiently operated, the most prosperous, and the best defended mission in the hemisphere.

In the opening sentences of his report Solís says: "This mission is so pretty and is in such a flourishing condition, both materially and spiritually, that I cannot find words or figures with which to express its beauty." However, as his report went on, page after page, he did seem to find the necessary words to support his premise. His observations covered such diverse subjects as the species of fish found in the San Antonio River, the beauty of the Indian women, the weight of the peaches grown in the mission orchards, and the vocal range of the Indian choir.

First, José de Solís noted the mission compound and activities engaged in, both within and without its walls. Of this he says:

> The structure consists of a perfect square of stone and lime, each side is two hundred and twenty varas long [six hundred and sixty feet] and has a door; there are towers in opposite corners, each one guarding its two sides. The dwellings of the Indians are built against the wall from five to six varas [fifteen to eighteen feet] in length and four [twelve feet] in width. Within each there is a little kitchen of four varas [twelve feet] in length, a chimney and loopholes which fall on the outside for defence against the enemy; there is an arched granary of stone and lime, [and] three cannon; there is a work-shop where woolen blankets and very good cotton and woolen cloth is woven. They make a great deal of the latter. They have a carpenter shop, an iron shop, a tailor shop, a furnace in which to burn lime and brick, and an irrigating ditch so large and carrying so much water that it seems like a small river, and it has a great number of fish in it. This canal waters many fertile fields, all of which are fenced in for more than a league. In these fields, they have

sown corn, brown beans, lentils, melons, watermelons, peaches, sweet potatoes, Irish potatoes, sugar cane. From all of these things they take large and abundant harvests, so that this mission gives food to others, and to the presidio of Orcoquisac and Los Adais. It has a garden in which they grow all kinds of vegetables and many fruit trees, especially peaches, one now and then of a pound in weight, little more or less.

Inspector Solís wrote that three hundred and fifty Indians of the Pampopa, Mesquite, Pastía, Canama, Tacame, Cana, Aguesalla, and Xaraname tribes lived within the mission's confines. About 110 of these were skilled in the handling of weapons, forty-five being armed with guns and sixty-five with bows and arrows and lances. For security purposes they regularly "patrolled in two files" inside the mission walls, while outside others rode horseback as sentinels.

Padre Solís noted that all of the Indians knew how to sing and dance "after the manner of the white people from the land outside," and "perhaps with more skill and beauty," and that the women, "except for an occasional coarse featured one, were comely and very graceful," that all were decently dressed, and that all the Indians had two suits of clothes—one for work days and the second for "feast days." The old men made arrows for the soldiers, while the old women spent their time catching fish for the padres. The younger women spun yarn and made cloth and sewed, and the boys and girls went to school and "prayed in their turn." Beds, placed high off the floor, used buffalo hides as mattresses, while sheets and blankets of cotton and wool served to insure warmth on cold nights. Occasionally the padres would become careless, and an Indian would slip off into the woods to worship pagans with his wild, un-Christian brother. But most of the time this was prevented, and those caught in this practice were severely punished.

They had been well taught in the Christian doctrine so José de Solís thought. All spoke the Spanish language except "those who came from the forest when grown and who have remained untamed and wild." Most were skilled in playing the guitar, the violin, or the harp, and, he added, "All have sonorous voices, and on Saturdays, each 19th day and the feast days of the Christ and the Most Holy Mary they take out their Rosaries, singing with four voices, soprano, alto, tenor, and bass, with musical accompaniment, and it is glorious to hear them."

Ten to twelve leagues to the south (in present Wilson County) the mission maintained a ranch known as "El Atascosita" or "Rancho de las Cabras (goats)," located on a high plateau on the west bank of the San Antonio River. Here, where all of the stock was kept, Padre Solís found "ten droves of mares, four droves of asses, thirty harnesses, 1,500 yoke of oxen for tilling the soil, 500 head of sheep and goats, and all necessary farming implements, such as plowshares, plows, hoes, axes, bars, etc." At El Atascosita, as at the mission, Solís noted that white overseers were not needed and that the Indians took complete charge of the ranch. The converts acted as mule drivers, masons, cowboys, and shepherds, and there was no need to employ anyone who did not belong to the mission.

Inspector Solís, not overlooking a thing, perceived that the banks of the San Antonio River were "very leafy and pleasant," being covered with many kinds of trees such as cottonwood, walnut, mesquite, pin oaks, and oaks. Types of fish abounding in the river were *barbos*, *pullones*, *pillontes*, sea-fish, sardines, and eels. Animals such as deer, wolves, coyotes, rabbits, wild cats, wild boars, and "now and then a (mountain) lion" roamed the woods, while overhead flew blue ducks, geese, turkeys, quail, partridges, hawks, and screech owls. These sights of nature pleased the inspector just as much as what he saw within the mission and at the ranch.

Padre José de Solís was very much impressed with San José Mission, its location, its inhabitants, its accomplishments, and its leaders. He left the mission on April 7, 1768, and submitted his glowing report to the Guardian of the College of Zacatecas the following summer.

Yet another visitor to San José has left an interesting bit of eighteenth century history concerning the mission. This man, Fray Juan Agustín Morfí, visited San José in late 1777. As those who visited before him, Padre Morfí was generous in his praise for the successful enterprise on the San Antonio. It was, he said, "the finest mission in this America and might well be called the *queen* of all others"— hence, comes the name by which it is commonly known today: the Queen of the Texas missions. Morfí also thought that it was the best constructed and the most easily defended of all the king's forts. Under the tutelage of Father Fray Pedro Ramirez, the mission had reached this "flourishing state."

Padre Morfí was particularly warm in his praise for the newly completed church, and well he should have been, for it is the one which today's generation still looks upon with awe and admiration. The first church of San José was completed on March 5, 1721, on the same day that the cornerstones were laid at the San Antonio missions of La Purisima, Concepción de Acuña, San Juan de Capistrano, and San Francisco de la Espada. The first church at San José served until 1768, when, according to José de Solís, it had been torn down and a new one started. On the second day of his visit, March 19, 1768, Padre Solís and Don Hugo de O'Conor (who apparently had a bit of Gaelic blood), governor and captain general of the Province of Texas, laid the first two stones for the structure. Since the holy edifice was completed by the time that Morfí was there late in 1777, he described it in detail,

> It has a beautiful cupola, though it is overcrowded with unnecessary ornaments. This building, because of its size, good taste, and beauty, would grace a large city as a parish church. The whole structure is admirably proportioned and strongly built of stone and mortar, chiefly out of a sandy limestone that is light and porous when freshly quarried but in a few days hardens and becomes one with the mortar, for which reason it is as useful for building as *tezontle*. This stone is secured from a quarry near the mission of Nuestra Señora de la Concepción. The facade is very costly because of the statues and ornaments with which it

was heavily decorated, detracting somewhat from its natural beauty. In the center, and immediately over the main entrance, a large balcony was constructed which gives much majesty to the building, and the effect would have been enhanced if the hexagonal window that illuminates the choir, and is the entrance, had been made to simulate a door. In a word, no one could have imagined that there were such good artists in so desolate a place.

The sacristy of the new church, the place where the divine services are celebrated for the time being, has a door that opens into the living quarters of the religious. It is a handsome and cheerful room, large and well decorated, with vaulted roof, good light, and everything in good taste.

The convent or living quarters for the missionaries has two stories with spacious galleries. The one on the second floor opens out on the flat roofs of the Indian quarters and is very convenient. The quadrants [sun dials] on vertical columns were set up there, made out of a species of limestone so soft when first brought from the quarry that it can be planed like wood but which, when exposed to the air, hardens and can be polished like marble. The figures of the facade of the church, the balustrade of the stairway of the convent, and an image of Saint Joseph that is on its pedestal, all were made more beautiful by the ease with which the stone is worked. There are enough rooms for the missionaries and for the convenience of a few guests, as well as the necessary offices for the religious, a large and well-ordered kitchen, a comfortable refectory, and a pantry. There is an armory where the guns, bows and arrows, and the lances are kept, with which to arm the neophytes in case of attack and to equip them as auxiliary troops in a campaign, in which case the mission provides them not only with arms, but with ammunition and supplies as well. In a separate room are kept the decorations and dresses with which the Indians bedeck themselves for their dances, introduced by the missionaries, now Spanish and now Mexican, that they might forget their native *mitotes* [pagan festivals].

In concluding his remarks about the church, Morfí gave several pertinent statistics. The tallest tower he said reached seventy-five feet in the air and the dome rose to a height of sixty feet. The church's dimensions were sixty-two feet across the front and 241 feet in length, including the monastery. He disclosed the depth of his cultural background in reporting that while the church was of "simple Moorish and Spanish origin," the stone carvings certainly reflected "the rich Renaissance influence of the Churrigueresque school of Spanish Baroque."

In summarizing the observations made by the visitors to San José during the eighteenth century, one cannot help being impressed by the emphasis placed upon soldiering and military preparedness at the mission. Although the mission was established primarily to convert the heathen Indians to Christianity and make them loyal and productive subjects of the king, military training and preparedness were an essential part of their life at the mission. Of course, the reasons for this are obvious. The mission was located in hostile Indian country several leagues from the Spanish military garrison at San Antonio. Too, military training fosters discipline and orderliness and promotes leadership—qualities necessary along with Christian conversion to make the Indian an effective member of the Spanish empire. In actuality San José mission was a small *presidio* and could (with some justification) be referred to as *Presidio* San Jose as well as Mission San Jose.

For instance, Father Ciprián in 1749 referred to San José as a "fortress" and remarked that the Apaches hesitated to attack it because of its strong walls and armed neophytes. Ten years later Governor Barrios called it the "best defended mission in Spanish America" and said that over one hundred neophytes bore arms, held target practice regularly, and made "admirable" soldiers and officers. Barrios also noted that the walls had loopholes for defense and that those neophytes who acted as soldiers had their own separate quarters and a swimming pool—a sort of a garrison within the mission compound. Solís, inspecting San José a decade later (1768) mentioned the fact that the mission had three cannon (which would qualify it to be a *presidio*), and that 110 of its neophytes were *skilled* at handling weapons, of which forty-five were armed with guns and sixty-five with bows and arrows and lances. The use of lances was practical only from horseback, a fact which suggests that the mission had men trained in all three branches of the service—cavalry, infantry, and artillery. Solís also noted and reported that security patrols were regularly used both inside and outside of the mission compound. Those on outside patrol were on horseback (probably lancers) and those on inside duty were foot soldiers. The inspector also mentioned that the old men of the mission made arrows for the soldiers. Morfí, visiting San José in 1777, stresses the fact that the mission was a military stronghold. He said that it was the "best constructed and most easily defended of all the king's *forts*," and that the *armory* was *well supplied* with guns, bows and arrows and lances. These instruments of war, Morfí said, were to be used to equip the neophytes "as auxiliary troops in a campaign" as well as for defense against an attack.

Thus, it appears that San José had a secondary role as an auxiliary *presidio*, and that the neophytes could and would be employed in offensive as well as defensive actions. This somewhat belligerent role for San José has been given little emphasis or publicity by mission historians.

In a time when building methods were rather crude and transportation of heavy materials difficult, much ingenuity, excellent supervision, and hard work went into the building of San José. The padres and Indians, working together, accomplished something of a miracle. The walls provide an excellent example. When they were built too high to be reached from the ground, earth was packed in the enclosure for the Indians to stand on to complete the work. When the spring line of the roof was reached, the earth was molded into the proper form and the arched roof was built. After the job had been completed, the earth inside of the structure was removed.

The walls around the mission were approximately six hundred feet long on each of the four sides, making it a perfect square. They rose to a height of from eight to twelve feet and ranged in thickness from fifty-eight to sixty-four inches. Building materials, obtained at nearby Mission Concepción, were a type of limestone and tufa.

The steps leading to the tower also testify to the ingenuity of the architects. A winding stairway, enclosed in a circular wall, led to the second floor. Each of the twenty-three steps in this stairway was hewn in a triangular shape from the heartwood of oak. The laborers set up the trunk of a large tree and cut steps eighteen inches wide into it to provide steps from the second floor to the tower's lookout window.

Two sculptural gems of San José which are worthy of note are the facade on the front door of the church and the celebrated "Rose Window" on the south side of the church. Carved from stone, they are filled with intricate detail which took not only talent, but also hours of toil. Above the door is a reproduction of the painting known as *Our Lady of Guadalupe*, which was completed near Mexico City in 1532. On the right and left sides of the door are Saint Joachim and Saint Anne, and above each is a heart representing the hearts of Mary and Joseph. On the upper part of the facade the artist carved a statue of Saint Joseph, the patron saint of the mission, and on each side of him were placed Saint Francis of Assisi and Saint Dominic. Originally the whole facade was surmounted by a richly carved cross below which was an image of the Sacred Heart of Jesus issuing flames of love and encircled by a crown of thorns. The ornately decorated doors which this facade surrounded were nine feet, six inches high and fourteen feet, eight inches wide, and they were ornately decorated.

The south window in the church has come to be known as the "Rose Window." Probably the carving on it was completed around 1790 or later, just as the missions were being secularized. The sculptor of this fine work, a "perpetual delight to the eye," was thought to be Pedro Huizar. The beautiful work of Huizar has been copied by countless painters and photographed innumerable times by both amateur and professional photographers. It is probably one of the best known and one of the most beautiful windows of its type in the world. It received its name "Rose Window" from either a beautiful legend concerning Pedro Huizar's love for a girl named Rosa or from the fact that its ornamentation bears some resemblance to the petals of a wild rose. (A rumor that the Rose Window was removed for a time and exhibited at the World's Fair in St. Louis, 1903-04, is without foundation.) Except for a little weathering, some unfortunate defacing, and a little new mortar around the edges, Pedro Huizar's work remains the same as when it was finished in the early 1790's. Besides sculpturing his beautiful piece of window art (and perhaps the facade on the church door), Huizar is also known as the person who surveyed the land adjoining the missions at San Antonio when they were secularized. Later his son, Juan Antonio Huizar, came into possession of the granary of San José, and it remained in the family for over a century.

San José's archives begin on September 7, 1777, when the book of baptisms, burials, and deaths was started. Officially the book is titled *Libro de Bautismos, Casmientos y Entierros pertenecientas a Mision San Jose*. The record of baptisms begins in September, 1777, and extends to the year 1824. The entries start with number 832, indicating that 831 Indians had been baptized prior to that time, and go up to number 1,211. Most of the baptisms after the year 1803 were performed for Spaniards, *mestizos* (offspring of a Spanish father and an Indian mother), and mulattoes (individuals born to one Negro and one white parent). The marriages cover the years 1778 to 1822, with the first entry being number 335 and the last 395 in the year 1796. Burial records cover the years 1781 to 1824. The first entry is number 847 and the last 1837. After 1804 the burials were mostly those of Spaniards, *mestizos*, and mulattoes. The book also reveals the names of some of the padres stationed at the mission. Padre Pedro Ramírez de Arrellano, president of all the missions in the Province of Texas, was in office in 1777 and he stayed at San José until his death in 1781. Other missionaries at San José were Padres José Francisco de la Cruz, 1782; José de la María de Salus, 1783-1789; José Augustín Falcón Mariano, 1784-1785; Pedro Noreño, Luis Gonzago Gomez, and

Manuel Gonz, 1786; Juan José Manuel Pedrazas, 1790, 1792-1794; José Mariano Rojos, 1791-1792; Josef Mariano Garza, 1793; Josef de Jesús Maria Cárdenas and José Manuel Pedrajo, 1793-1800; Josef Aguilar, 1798; Bernardino Vallejo, 1799-1810; Juan María Sepulveda, 1811; Manuel María Trexes, 1818-1819; Manuel Muro, 1819-1820; and José Antonio Díaz de Léon, 1820-1824.

Both José de Solís and Juan Morfí saw San José Mission at the height of its popularity in the 1760's and 1770's. In these two decades it was functioning at peak performance—the actors on the stage little suspected that the end of the mission system was fast approaching; however, population figures give mute testimony that the mission was withering. At the end of 1783 San José had only 128 Indians within its walls. By 1786 the figure had grown to 189, but it fell to 114 two years later in 1788. The year 1790 saw an increase to 144, a figure which decreased to 106 the following year. In 1794, when the mission was secularized, only ninety-nine neophytes lived at San José, once the home of over three hundred Christianized Indians.

When France ceded Louisiana to Spain in 1772, a new approach to the whole mission system was taken by Spanish officials. One of the tenets of this new attitude was that the missions were no longer necessary for the defense of the region. Missionaries could think about Christianizing heathens if they wanted, but political officials had to think about the problem of cutting costs and of over-all national defense. Drastic changes in the system were contemplated as early as 1778, but no action was taken. When Father Fray Manuel Silva became commissary and prefect of the missions of the College of Zacatecas in 1790, he made an inspection tour of the Texas missions and recommended that the number of missions in the San Antonio area be reduced to two. Objections by both the city officials and the mission padres were raised to this planned reduction, but they went for naught. As a matter of fact, the government went further than Silva's recommendations and ordered all missions secularized and removed from the Spanish system of colonial enterprise. San José's turn for secularization came on July 16, 1794, with the arrival of the governor of the Province of Texas, Don Manuel Muñoz.

Upon his arrival at San José, Muñoz ordered the priest in charge, Father Fray José Manuel Pedrajo, to summon all of the neophytes and turn over to them the temporal property of the mission. Ninety-six persons were listed to receive property—a far cry from the number who would have been eligible in the 1760's and 1770's. The inventory list of the property disposed of is of interest, for it gives some indication of what material wealth remained at San José in 1794. Items inventoried for distribution to the Christianized Indians included: sixteen axes, one chisel, two crowbars, four bucksaws, one hand saw, one English saw, eighteen adzes, and fifty-one pairs of shears. Animals on the list were: fourteen yoke of oxen, thirteen yoke of "young bullocks," thirty-four milk cows and their calves, and 125 horses. A completely equipped blacksmith shop was distributed along with ninety sacks of wheat from the granary and a branding iron; three fully equipped looms, five pairs of cards, and 575 pounds of raw wool. The corn and sugar cane planted in the fields was likewise divided.

After the distribution of the temporal property, a survey and subdivision of the mission's farming lands had to be made. On July 22 and 23 the land was divided among the Indians by Governor Muñoz. In addition to the land and temporal property, the Indians also received title to the buildings of San José, except for the church and fifteen acres of land. Thus, in the short period of eight days San José was converted from a mission with extensive holdings in land and livestock, valuable temporal property, and a labor force of about a hundred families to a simple parish church and fifteen acres of land. Within three quarters of a century the most successful mission in Texas had been planted, had sprouted, matured, withered and died.

Only one other item remained to be settled before

secularization was completed—money owed to the mission had to be collected and debts owed by the mission had to be paid. Padre Pedrajo was in a position to determine these money matters, but he was sent to Refugio on another matter and did not make his financial report until almost a year later (June 12, 1795). The mission owed 2,230 pesos to three individuals named Angel Navarro, Joaquín Flores, and Domingo de Otón. On the other hand thirty-eight persons were in debt to the mission and owed in the aggregate 6,118.75 pesos. Governor Muñoz waited two years for instructions from Mexico City on the disposition of these claims. In 1797 he was finally told to collect the money owed the mission and to settle the claims against the mission.

The fact that San José was secularized did not mean that the padres were inactive, that they had de-emphasized their Christianizing, or that the mission complex had completely deteriorated. The Indians still owned the land; the Catholic Church owned the mission property; and both the priests and the Indians still had living quarters within the mission complex. The famous American explorer and soldier, Zebulon Montgomery Pike (who later would be killed leading an assault against Canada in 1814) stopped at San José on June 7, 1807. He noted in his diary that he was "received in a friendly manner by the priest of the mission." Manuel de Salcedo found twenty-nine Indian men, twenty-six Indian women, and nine men and six women of Spanish descent living at San José in June, 1809.

Apparently, after secularization, the church purchased a large amount of land from the government for Salcedo remarked that the San José church owned a large piece of land bounded on the south by Arroyo de la Piedra, on the north by the ranch owned by one Valdés, on the east by the San Antonio River, and on the west by the Medina River. This was in addition to the fifteen acres kept by the church at the time of secularization and the eleven sitios (48,708 acres) on the Medina River purchased from the crown in 1766.

However, unfortunate times fell on San José and its inhabitants during the decade from 1810 to 1820. In October, 1813, Governor Antonio Martínez reported on the disposition he had made of five guns that Lieutenant Colonel Don Ygnacio Perez had captured from Comanche Indians. Three of these weapons were sold to the *vecinos* of San Jose, "who had no means of defense." Also, they had no money and had to pay for the guns from the corn they had just harvested. (Eighteen pesos was the price involved in the transaction.) Padre Bernardine Vallejo surveyed the mission early in 1815 and listed its population at 109—forty-nine Indians and sixty Spaniards. He commented that the Indians to whom the property had been given when the mission was secularized were "practically destitute." He hastened to add that the religious services were not a financial burden to them as the priest was paid by the royal treasurer. The chapel, he wrote, was in a "fair state of preservation" and was well provided with all that was needed for religious services. Even though the archives of the missions were destroyed in the abortive filibustering Gutierrez-Magee expedition which captured San Antonio in 1813, San José itself was unharmed. Then, as if to cap off the unhappy decade, a mission Indian was killed in March, 1819, when the mission was attacked by a group of marauding Comanches. In addition, a fight that had erupted between the padres of San José and the officers of the government came to a head during the last years of the decade. In September, 1819, Governor Martínez wrote a scathing report on "the Most Blessed Minister, Friar Francisco Trexes," the priest in charge of San José. He thought the priest to be "of little or no use" because "he has treated these poor curacies with little charity, and his arrogant and quarrelsome character has created no few inconveniences for this government." The inhabitants of San José claimed that Trexes had taken such items as two millstones, one large kettle, one steelyard, one flagstone clock, and one chest away from them and sold the items for his own personal benefit.

Little information is available on San José in the Mexican period of Texas history, from 1821 to 1836. As the sparks of the Texas revolution were being fanned into flames in the fall of 1835, General Stephen F. Austin was leading his Texian volunteer army toward San Antonio to wrest the strategic spot from the Mexicans. The Texians were active, casting about for good fortifications in which to house the troops and defend themselves if necessary. It was five o'clock on Friday, October 23, 1835, when two of the most colorful frontiersmen ever to grace the Texas scene sat down to draft a report to the Father of Texas, Stephen F. Austin. The two were James Bowie and James W. Fannin, Jr., both of whom had less than six months left in their eventful lives. They were describing to Austin the condition of the missions near San Antonio and their possible use as troop billets. Their headquarters was Mission Espada. At San José they found only one family, no corn, and only a small crop of peas. The corn had failed because the dam had broken early in the season and the crop had been abandoned. The mission was "in a dilapidated state," but even so it had "fine quarters for the men"; however, water was too remote and the Texians would be "too much at the mercy of the enemy," so they decided not to use Mission San José. The crumbling buildings of San José seem to have stood in mute silence as Santa Anna stormed the walls of the nearby Alamo to deal death to Bowie and his comrades and as the Mexican army dispatched in cold blood at Goliad James W. Fannin and most of his command.

Throughout the Republic of Texas years, San José served intermittently as quarters for soldiers of the Texas army. In 1840 William S. Fisher, Lieutenant Colonel of the First Infantry, housed one hundred sixty frontier Texians there. In her *Memoirs*, Mary A. Maverick tells how Isimanica, chief of the Comanches, and approximately three hundred braves approached San

José and Fisher's contingent shortly after the Council House Fight. Isimanica and his warriors "with fearless daring bantered the soldiers for a fight, but Captain William D. Redd, in command because of the illness of Fisher, remained calm and refused to fight. Eventually the Indians left San José and did not return.

During the 1840's San José was graced by several distinguished visitors. William Bollaert, an Englishman who arrived in Texas in 1842, found time to visit the mission in 1843 and record his observations for posterity. He found eight or ten Mexican families "to whom mass was occasionally said" living within its walls. The church was "still in good preservation" but was "full of bats' nests." Only one split bell was left in the tower and the "images of the staints and other ornamental parts" had been "sadly mutilated by the soldiery during the wars." He commented on the "exquisite work and labour" which had been bestowed on the door and window of the vestry.

Seth Eastman, an artist, was at San José in August, 1849, with forty-seven soldiers, eight wagons, nine teamsters, and one wagon master in his party. Even though he got his facts wrong in writing a brief historical sketch of the mission, he did take time to make several excellent drawings, one of which is preserved in his *Sketchbook*. He was absolutely correct when he wrote that the mission was "going to ruins."

John Russell Bartlett confirmed Eastman's observation when he visited San José in 1851. Still, he thought San José was in a better state of preservation than the other missions. Bartlett mentioned the elaborate carvings on the door and window, adding that the weather had done much to destroy the figures and that the soldiers had fired many times at them, at once improving their "skill in arms" and showing their "contempt for the Mexican belief." He mentions the red and blue "sort of stencilling of colors" on the front of the church and the frescoes on the interior walls which had been destroyed by dampness. The altar, he noted, had been stripped of its ornamentations, but it did not matter because the Mexicans of the neighborhood were poor and could not "often afford the fifty dollars charged by the San Antonio priests for officiating;" thus the temple was seldom used for religious purposes. The only inhabitant Bartlett found was an American who farmed the lands adjoining the mission and lived in the priests' quarters.

But San José as a Catholic and historical site was not to be relegated to oblivion. John M. Odin, the architect of its resurrection, was sent to Texas in 1840 as Vice-Prefect Apostolic of the Catholic Church. Odin interested himself in Catholic activities and petitioned the Congress of the Republic of Texas for the return to the Catholic Church of all church buildings, missions, and adjoining lands which had belonged to the Catholic Church under the Spanish government. His efforts were crowned with success in a law enacted on January 13, 1841. Mission San José was included in the enactment. Odin had visited San José in September of 1840 and was captivated by its beauty and its state of preservation. It would be a pity, he thought, if the mission fell into "the hands of Protestants." Odin felt that it could easily be made into a college, a seminary, or boys' school.

The opportunity to convert his belief into action came in June, 1858, when Odin went to St. Vincent, Pennsylvania. The purpose of his visit to this quaint college town was to convince the Benedictine Archabbot, Boniface Wimmer, to establish a convent at San José. Odin had five hundred acres of land and the buildings to offer; and if the Archabbot would provide financial assistance, Mission San José could be rebuilt. Again Odin's persuasiveness won out, and the Benedictines accepted the offer. On July 1, 1859, three priests and two brothers, all under the direction of Prior Alto Hoermann, set out for San Antonio. They worked hard to expand the faith and rebuild the mission, but two major problems which eventually caused their withdrawal beset them.

They were from the North and were naturally suspected by those Texians with Southern sentiments, a feeling which greatly impeded their religious work. The second problem had to do with the restoration of San José itself. Exposure to the elements had weakened the mission's walls and the "stone floor harbored all kinds of vermin." When the rains came, the missionaries "were often drenched in bed, and in the morning water stood ankle-deep in the rooms." Moreover, after the war came in 1861, it was impossible to acquire either laborers or building materials. The Benedictines labored on against great odds until 1867, when the decision came from Pennsylvania to withdraw from Texas and San José. They were gone by the end of the following year.

Within a few years the reconstruction work that the Benedictines had accomplished was erased by the elements, souvenir hunters, and vandals. In 1873 (although some sources say 1868) the north wall of the church collapsed taking down with it the beautiful dome and the cupola. The collapse was caused, some say, by treasure hunters digging for what they thought was a cache of gold hidden beneath the walls of the church; this, coupled with the weakened condition of the wall itself, caused the venerable structure to buckle and fall.

In the same year, that part of the church was reduced to a heap of stone and mortar. Five years after the Benedictines had departed, another Catholic order, the Holy Cross Fathers of Big Bend, Indiana, took over the project of trying to restore and revive the mission. The Holy Cross Fathers labored until 1888; then like the Benedictines before them, they gave up the project; and San José again was abandoned to the elements, the weeds, and the bats—a deserted historical site on the winding San Antonio.

For the next thirty-four years, until 1922, the former queen of the missions remained practically unfunded, untouched, and unwanted. In 1922 the Redemptionist Fathers took over San José and operated it for nine years, when it was turned over to the Franciscan Fathers of the Province of the Sacred Heart of St. Louis. The Franciscans came at the invitation of Archbishop Arthur J. Drossaerts and built a new Friary on a three-acre tract of land east of the old convent. This building was dedicated on October 24, 1931, after which Father Bonaventure Alerding, newly appointed Superior of the Community and Pastor of the parish, took charge. The church is still operated under the Archdiocese of San Antonio.

Action to restore the original San José to its former splendor was begun as early as 1917 by the De Zavala Chapter of the Daughters of the Republic of Texas and by the Texas Historic Landmarks Association. The extent of their success is not known, but a donation was secured by the Archdiocese of San Antonio and some rebuilding was done. The De Zavala Daughters "propped up the beautiful front doorway to keep the arch from falling, repaired the roof of the sacristy, and tried to retain all stones and woodwork in place." Serious and successful restoration seems to have been actively commenced in the 1930's. The church of San José was restored beginning in 1934 by the Archdiocese of San Antonio and the Works Progress Administration of the Federal Government. It was completed and rededicated on April 18, 1937. The San Antonio Conservation Society set the granary in good order, while Bexar County and the Works Progress Administration restored the compound walls.

In a document dated June 1, 1941, San José Mission was designated as a National Historic Site by the United States Department of the Interior. This was done after an agreement had been reached between the Texas State Parks Board, the Archdiocese of San Antonio, and the United States Government for the ownership and operation of the site.

Today the Queen of the Texas Missions is officially known as San José Mission State Park and is administered by the Texas Parks and Wildlife Department. As previously noted, much of the old mission complex has been restored, thanks to the Catholic church, Bexar County, the United States government, the State of Texas, the San Antonio Conservation Society and several other local historical groups.

Because of the efforts of these organizations, a visitor to San José can still see many things as they appeared in the prime years of the mission. The doors of the church still hang on the original hand-wrought hinges. One may still climb the original winding stair of hand-hewn live oak logs to the tower that served both as a belfry and as a lookout post used for spotting hostile Indians. The Rose Window is still as beautiful as ever, even though slightly worn by age. The exquisite carvings of the facade are still visible although many of the figures are missing. The prefecture, the granary, the mill, the double walls of the mission with the neophyte quarters, the corner bastion, the gate bastion, and the old mill have all been rebuilt. The *Convento*, the living quarters and offices for the clergy, has been purposely left in ruins to show the structural beauty of the arches. The Soldiers' Quarters likewise have been purposely left in ruins in order to present an example of the compound's walls before restoration.

Truly the restoration of San José has been remarkable; and through the efforts of many people, an important epoch of early Texas history has been preserved for future generations.

The story of San José would not be complete without mentioning the legends that have come to be associated with the mission down through the years. A legend has been defined as "a narrative based partly on history but chiefly on popular tradition." The history of many famous sites is intertwined with strange beliefs, legends, and traditions that tend to romanticize, add an aura of suspense to and/or create an unusual interest in a building or an area. Two beautiful and romantic but unfortunately tragic legends are associated with San José; one concerns the famous Rose Window and the other the bells of the church tower.

First, the legend of the most famous mission window in the world. Pedro Huizar (sometimes spelled Huicar and Huisar), the handsome young Spaniard who designed and sculptured the Rose Window, was a descendant of the architect who designed the world-famous Alhambra, a Moorish castle and stronghold in Spain. An adventurer at heart, Pedro decided to come to New Spain, gain fame and fortune as a sculptor, then send to Spain for his village sweetheart, the beautiful Rosa. After reaching Mexico City, Pedro learned of the beauty of San José located on the San Antonio River and determined to journey there and link his fame to that of the famous mission by offering his talent as a sculptor to the padres. He arrived at San José in the late 1780's and was assigned the task of decorating the window on the south wall of the church. The padres took for granted that the young Spaniard would carry out a religious theme. But Pedro was young; he was in love; and he was in a new country full of adventure, romance, and the zest for living. He determined to dedicate this window to Rosa and make it the most beautiful piece of artistry in the world. Then, with his fame established, he would send for Rosa and marry her in the Mission of San José in the shadow of "his" window.

As Pedro carved, his whole being was full of love for Rosa. Into his sculpturing he poured his heart and soul, working from sunrise to sunset. As the window took shape, it symbolized all the grace and beauty of his loved one. His first great work about completed, Pedro wrote for Rosa to take the next ship to Mexico. Soon she was on her way to the new world. As the last rose was being shaped, and as Pedro was visualizing Rosa standing beside him and taking her vows as his wife, a hand was gently laid upon his shoulder. It was the hand of a padre who told him the tragic news of his sweetheart's death at sea. Pedro was beside himself with grief and vowed to devote the rest of his life to the church. For the next twenty years Pedro Huizar painted and sculptured for the Mission of San José and it is thought that

many of the beautiful carvings of the mission's facade
were the result of his skillful hands guided by a broken
heart.

The second legend, like the first, is built around love
and tragedy and concerns the mission bells. It seems
that a young Spanish nobleman, Don Luis Angel de
León, full of love and zeal for his God and king, wanted
to do some worthy act for them in the New World. He
would only remain a short time in New Spain, for he
had promised to marry Teresa, a high born maiden of
Old Castile. Don Angel came to San Antonio and was
stationed at the *presidio* there. The memory of Teresa
buoyed up his spirits and gladdened his days of loneliness on the frontier. Soon the time would come when
he could return to Spain and marry the beautiful Castilian maiden. He was scheduled to leave on the next
expedition back to Spain, but this was not to be. A sudden raid by the Apaches, a running fight, and an arrow
pierced the young nobleman's heart as he rode near the
mission of San José. Don Angel's body was brought
to San José and he was buried in the mission cemetery.

The news of the young nobleman's death reached
Teresa as she had gathered with others to witness the
casting of the bells for the famous mission. As the
molten mass was flowing into the molds a sudden in-
spiration seized the distraught maiden. She removed
the gold ring from her finger and the cross from around
her neck that Don Angel had given her and flung them
into the molten metal. Those near her heard her mur-
mur sadly, "Oh bells, you go to look upon the grave
where my dear one lies. Take with you these treasured
relics of the one that I love. It may be that when you
softly ring the Angelus for the first time above his far-
off grave he will hear and know that I was faithful and
loved him until the end."

The fair maiden's heart was broken, and gradually
she wasted away, pining for her dead lover. One evening, as the sun was setting and the western sky was
ablaze with color, Teresa, thinking that the rays of the

setting sun were shining upon her loved one's grave, suddenly smiled and whispered: "The bells, it is the Angelus! and Don Angel hears!" With these words the fair Teresa fell lifeless to the ground, her eyes fixed on the western horizon—she had joined her Don Angel.

> Every morn at break of dawn,
> And then at close of day,
> Sound ringing clearly on the air,
> The bells of San José.

San Juan de Capistrano

Mission San Juan de Capistrano

San Juan Capistrano

by

Ben Procter

The eighteenth century was a time of challenge for
New Spain, of quickening activity, of arduous devotion
to church and state, and yet of tension and foreboding.
For almost two hundred years a relatively small number
of men had risked their lives to conquer Spain's enemies, to expand its empire, to magnify its glory and
wealth. Some were rugged nobles or soldiers of fortune
who had helped conquer the Moors and were looking for
new dominions; others were dedicated friars who wanted to expand the realm of Christendom, to baptize the
heathen and save his soul. But to many the new world
offered a certain freedom, an unrestricted existence
which the authoritarianism of the church and state
often excluded.

First had come the conquistadors, men of courage
and stamina, of ruthless determination — arrogant,
proud warriors, humble only before their God and their
king. To them the new world was a glorious adventure
amidst heathen savages, fabulous treasures, and
strange, unknown vistas. Whether across swamp or
desert, mountain or plain, they endured and overcame,
carrying before them the cross and banner of Spain.
Such men as Cortés, Pizarro, Coronado, and De Soto
were, as Herbert Bolton put it, "armored knights upon
armored horses." And even though an obscure, lonely
fate might await them, there was no terrain too insur-
mountable, no land too remote, no climate too insuffer-
able.

With unbelievable rapidity they penetrated the wilderness, spreading Spanish civilization—its mores, institutions, language, and religion—in the wake of their

onslaught. From strategic bases at Havana, San Juan, and Santo Domingo they advanced on Mexico, then southward to Central America, then onward to Peru and to even greater triumphs and riches. Here, for a time, was their major area of concentration, their most notable achievement. Back to the coffers of the king flowed gold and silver and precious stones, back to Spain drifted tales of heroism and daring which excited the imagination of Spanish writers and artists, which triggered others to crave a similar way of life, while across South and Central America emerged the evidences of their success—cities and towns, schools and universities, churches and monasteries, haciendas and ranches. By 1600 Spanish officials and priests dominated some 5,000,000 natives, ministering to their needs and conducting their daily affairs.

Once life had become routine, the conquistadors had moved northward, past Mexico City, past Sonora, Coahuila, and Chihuahua to the northern borderlands. Here was a frontier of unknown quantity, dangerous to enter, expensive to conquer, difficult to defend. Yet here was California where, according to legend, Amazon Queen Califía ruled over other statuesque maidens. Somewhere in desert wastes lay the Gran Quivira, its golden walls glistening, its turquoise-studded doors beckoning them. And for hundreds of miles north of the Rio Grande stretched the "Kingdom of the Texas" where Indians used emeralds for arrowheads and feasted on shaggy, humpbacked cattle. For these bold men here indeed was a new frontier that stirred their curiosity, that drove them to super human feats of strength and endurance, that would give them no rest until they unlocked its mysteries.

Not far behind them, however, were robed padres, men of the Jesuit, Dominican, and Franciscan orders, men who were also a conquering force. But unlike the conquistadors they sought the Indian's soul as well as his body; theirs was a religious urge to save him for this world as well as for the next, not to break his spirit or destroy him. Together with philanthropists and reformers they denounced the *encomienda* system which had first been used to Christianize, control, and utilize the Indian. How disillusioning it was to see men convert a trusteeship over innocent natives into a method of virtual enslavement. So in comparison to the conquistadors and *encomenderos*, the rather gentle padres were not nearly so impressive, so dramatic, so awe-inspiring. But what they accomplished was. For on the far northern frontier it was they who initiated the long, drawn-out process of civilizing the Indian, first teaching him a sedentary form of existence, then converting him to Christianity. It was they who expanded the realms of Spain and Christendom, who walked naked into the wilderness.

The mission was their point of contact, an unshakable faith in God their intangible power. At each new station the padres (the Franciscans usually worked in pairs, the Jesuits alone) focused on the pueblo or Indian village, for it represented the basis of their existence—the extension of Christianity with necessary manpower to sustain them. But equally important were a church and chapel. The neophytes must understand discipline, they must learn to humble themselves before both God and man. And what better discipline was there than the Church—the bells at sunrise calling them to mass, the silence of the devotion, repeating prayers, the Creed, and the Rosary in unison, chanting the Salve or the Alabado? During the day the padres worked with the neophytes in the fields, directing the construction of irrigation ditches or the cultivation of crops. Just as often they drilled them in stock raising, weaving, tanning, or other industrial arts, crafts which were essential to maintaining economic self-sufficiency and which slowly raised the Indian above his barbaric past. To break the monotony of frontier life, of infinite discipline and rigorous training, there were religious holidays and fiestas resplendent in pomp and pageantry, usually followed by a variety of games, horse racing, and, if conditions permitted, a bull fight or rodeo. Equally exciting were periodic elections whereby the neophytes selected their own civil and military officials —modeled after the Spanish—to govern them.

But if this were not enough, if the Indians ran away or rebelled, if they were unwilling to sacrifice their freedom for economic security and the promise of salvation, then the padres relied upon the military. In or near each mission there were four to six soldiers. It was their duty to protect the mission against Indian attack, to bring back runaways, to punish the recalcitrant, indeed to remind the neophytes that in breaking God's laws there was worldly pain.

So by the eighteenth century the Spanish method of conquest had changed somewhat, now that the northern borderlands were a major frontier. Expeditions such as Coronado's had proven too expensive, the benefits most unsatisfactory and unrewarding. To any new request to explore or push into new areas government responses were usually negative, reasons varying as widely as individuals. Only if there were both political and religious advantages to be gained or a foreign threat to Spanish domain would there arise any feverish activity, any sustained momentum. With the gradual extinction of the *encomienda* system the mission became the dominant frontier institution, the most prominent outpost for both church and state. And as for the men of the different religious orders, they now assumed a role hitherto unrealized. Instead of being followers, trying to sustain or remold what the conquistadors had conquered or crushed, they were leaders, the foremost agents of the empire.

Nor were there many men who had the spiritual conviction, the dedication, indeed the physical stamina and inner strength to endure the missionary frontier. By mule or horse or on foot the padres moved northward into the lands of the Apaches and the Comanches, into areas that soldiers feared to enter. And there, with death ever present, they established their outposts *entre infieles* for Spain. Every baptism might be a portent of doom (if the person should die suddenly or become mysteriously ill). At any time a jealous sachem or medicine man might direct his followers toward their naturally destructive bents—the whiz of the arrow, the dreaded fire in the night, the petrifying war whoop. Just as often the frontier itself was the worst adversary, the cold and hunger and dust and heat. But possibly worse than any of these was the loneliness they suffered, lost in a wilderness of ignorant savages, in a voiceless land of parched deserts, silent peaks, and endless prairies.

What an incredible, almost unbelievable accomplishment it was—a long, thin line of missions and presidios stretching from Texas to California, protecting Spain's far-flung empire, a handful of men conquering and civilizing a savage land. Yet it happend. The Mission San Juan Capistrano still exists to remind us.

It was not until the late seventeenth century that Spain decided to colonize Texas—and then it was because of French encroachment. In 1684 La Salle, in trying to establish a colony at the mouth of the Mississippi, had missed his designated site and landed at Matagorda Bay. Mutiny, disease and Indian attack soon eliminated the temporary French Colony at Fort St. Louis, but the Spanish had to make sure. After all, the French were aggressive empire builders, eager to outdo the Spanish in controlling the continent. Already they had pushed their way from Canada to the Great Lakes, then south and west into the hinterlands. Even now they were colonizing the West Indies (once considered Spain's exclusive territory) and were sending corsairs to raid Spanish possessions. Somewhere the Spanish must take a stand, such aggressions must not go unchecked, for the English and Russians were also becoming much bolder in areas where Spain was concerned.

So from 1686 to 1689 the Spanish focused on Texas. Three expeditions commanded by Captain Alonso de León hunted for survivors of La Salle's ill-fated colony.

Stories of white men living with the Indians and of armed Frenchmen trying to induce the natives to join them were investigated. Anxious to be among the Tejas or Asinai Indians "for the immediate extension of the Gospel," padres like Franciscan Damian Massanet emphasized the need for missions to curb foreign intrigue. Yet equally persuasive to the viceroy and other government officials was León's report—the rich kingdom of Texas abounding in wild game, blessed with a salubrious climate, inhabited by intelligent, friendly, even docile Indians who had already received some religious instruction and were desiring more. "Certainly it is a pity," León lamented, "that people so rational, who plant crops and know that there is a God, should have no one to teach them the Gospel, especially when the province of Texas is so large and fertile and has so fine a climate."

Because of such reasoning and inducements the Spanish decided to occupy Texas, to establish their first outpost *entre infieles*. Late in March, 1690, Leon and Massanet, leading an expedition of one hundred and ten soldiers and twelve padres, moved northward across the Rio Grande and then eastward. By May 22 they contacted the Tejas near the Neches River where with gifts and showmanship they immediately won them over. Then they set in motion their process of civilizing —appointing the Indian chief as governor, baptizing his subjects and having them swear allegiance to the king, instructing them in the discipline of the church, having the neophytes construct the padres' lodgings and a church in the midst of the largest Indian village. On June 1 all was ready. In a special High Mass, Father Massanet officially blessed the Mission San Francisco de los Tejas.

But despite this auspicious beginning Massanet and his colleagues soon became disenchanted; three years on the Texas frontier saw to that. Being hundreds of miles from civilization left them extremely vulnerable, unable at any time to rely on reinforcements or help if difficulties arose. Within a short time raiding Indians practically eliminated the mission herds. Then droughts and floods alternated in destroying two successive crops (also shattering León's chamber of commerce illusion of a healthful climate). In desperation the padres shortened their rations to one small corn cake twice a day; pathetic Indian women begged even for a piece of cowhide; children starved; and disease spread rapidly through the weakened ranks.

Increasingly the Tejas looked upon the padres with deep suspicion. What had caused the havoc, this plague upon their land? With telling effect medicine men pointed to lethal baptismal waters, to the mysterious, terrifying epidemic, to the parallel of Spanish arrival and ensuing hard times. So bitter did the situation become that the Tejas chief warned the Spanish to leave, otherwise they would die.

Actually Massanet and his associates had already decided to abandon San Francisco de los Tejas. There was no longer any reason to stay. For the past year the Indians had become indifferent to the padres' wishes, refusing to adhere to church doctrine. In the mornings they would not attend mass. When one of their number died, they performed their own heathen rituals. And instead of accepting only the Christian God, they acknowledged two, one who gave the Spanish so many material blessings, the other who made the corn grow, the rain fall, the sun shine. Without a sufficient military force (the garrison consisted of nine soldiers), the padres could not protect themselves, much less enforce their orders.

On October 25, 1693, Massanet applied the torch to three years of effort and strenuous labor, to his most cherished dream, and dejectedly retreated to civilization. Forty days of wandering in the Texas wilderness, days of thirst and hunger in rugged terrain, further emphasized the futility of the venture. It would take far more than a token force and half-hearted government support to occupy the northern borderlands successfully. But for the moment such an enterprise was too expensive, and besides, the French threat had subsided.

For the next twenty years the Spanish were, in the main, apathetic toward Texas. But there was sporadic activity which eventually caused them to show interest and register concern. Franciscan friars, especially from the colleges of Querétaro and Zacatecas, fervently desired to work among the Asinai or Tejas Indians again. Yet despite their continued agitation, government officials were unresponsive. But anticipating a reversal of policy, the Franciscans pushed the frontier northward from Coahuila, establishing by 1703 three missions and a presidio on the Rio Grande (stepping stones necessary to advance). At the same time the French decided to carry out La Salle's scheme of colonizing the Lower Mississippi River Valley. In 1699 they established a fort at Biloxi and considered placing one at Mobile Bay after an unsuccessful move against the new Spanish outpost at Pensacola. After that, rumors throughout New Spain were persistent and disturbing. It was reported that Frenchmen were roaming widely both east and west of the Mississippi, building up Indian alliances, securing the fur trade, ever watchful for Spanish frailties. Some French *coureur de bois* were supposed to have contacted the Pawnee somewhere along the Red or Arkansas rivers, preparing for an attack on Santa Fé. Nor would it be long until they would appear along the Rio Grande and in Coahuila. Since nothing concrete materialized, however, the Spanish remained inactive, but nervous.

Such passiveness, indeed such inertia, was more than the Franciscan friar, Father Hidalgo, could bear. For years he had begged to be allowed to return to Texas where he had been with Massanet. How could he carry out the will of God, how could he save the heathen, if his superiors kept him hamstrung? Irritated to the point of exasperation, he decided to take matters into his own hands, if possible, to force the issue. On January 11, 1711, he wrote letters to the French Governor, LaMothe

Cadillac of Louisiana, and to fellow Franciscans, asking for their cooperation in establishing a mission among the Tejas.

When Cadillac finally received Hidalgo's note, he enthusiastically endorsed it. For months he had hoped to enlarge French trade in the Southwest. Now was his chance to break New Spain's strict commercial monopoly. To head a twenty-five man expedition he chose, after careful deliberation, the presidio captain at Biloxi, Louis Juchereau de St. Denis, a resourceful frontiersman who had lived among the Tejas and spoke their language, and yet a man who had the polish and finesse of a diplomat, a man who knew success. In 1713 he instructed St. Denis to find Hidalgo, to help him minister to the Indians, and, most important, to establish a trading post near the Red River.

After searching for Hidalgo for more than a year, after braving a thousand miles of wilderness and hostile Indians and an indifferent climate, St. Denis reached San Juan Bautista, the presidio two leagues south of the Rio Grande, where the elusive priest was last reported. And what an effect his arrival had. Presidio Captain Don Diego Ramón received him cordially but secretly sent a messenger to Mexico City for instructions. When Hidalgo heard the news, he was overjoyed; his dream was becoming a reality. Deeply grateful he thanked God for sending the French, thereby giving him a return passport to the Asinais. But the viceroy and his court were highly suspicious, especially after ordering St. Denis to Mexico City and questioning him. Although apparently open and frank with the Spanish, he did not volunteer information, and at times he seemed to be rather secretive. It was what he did not say, what he would not confirm, that bothered them. Obviously the French were hoping to open trade routes as far as the Rio Grande, and possibly they were sincere in offering aid to the East Texas missions. But were not their plans more complicated, more Machiavellian?

Meeting on August 22, 1715, the viceroy and his officers resolved the question—Spain would reoccupy Texas immediately. Such a move would eliminate all doubts, would placate fears of foreign aggression, would gratify the Franciscans. Immediately the viceroy appointed Domingo Ramón, the grandson of the presidio captain at San Juan Bautista, as captain of the expedition, and named St. Denis as second in command. Nor was the choice of the ingratiating Frenchman surprising. He could be most valuable. After all, he had recently been in Texas; he knew the language; and the Indians liked him. Besides, just a few weeks before he had married into a prominent Spanish family.

Late in March, 1716, the Ramon-St. Denis *entrada* or expedition moved northward from Saltillo, and like previous Spanish invasion forces moving into the northern borderlands it experienced untold hardships. Guiding seventy-five people including twenty-five soldiers, nine padres, and six women through a wilderness was hard enough but transporting all the necessary equipment for four missions plus herding a thousand cattle, sheep, and goats was even more difficult. After crossing the Rio Grande, they moved across a desert-like terrain of mesquite and cactus and sun-baked soil, the heat and humidity sapping their strength every step of the way. By May 14 they reached San Pedro Spring and the San Antonio River (within two years the Spanish would establish the mission outpost of San Antonio there) where they rested for a few days. Then they pressed doggedly eastward, past the flooded Colorado and Brazos rivers, past the confusingly similar wooded streams of East Texas, until on June 12 they contacted four chiefs of the Asinais. So rugged had been the journey that thirty-four of the sixty-four oxen had died from exhaustion. But it had been worth it to the padres, especially Hidalgo. He had at last returned home.

For almost a month the Spanish were unusually successful. At first they attended what seemed to be interminable feasts, the Asinais killing the proverbial fatted calf for the return of the prodigals. In turn, Ramón distributed gifts profusely among the populace, while to impress them even more his soldiers fired salvos to salute a chief or to signify some gala occasion. Not to be outdone, the padres performed solemn, elaborate rituals, stirring the Indians to reverence and awe. These measures were effective. Overwhelming them with affection, the Asinais kissed their hands, attended High Mass, and asked to be baptized.

At the same time, however, Ramón was well aware of what had happened to the last colonizing venture, so he cautiously laid plans for permanent settlement. In many Tejas villages he organized the populace according to the Spanish method, appointing their leaders to such positions as governor, captain, alcalde, and aguacil. While instructing his men to help the padres build temporary shelters and control the Indians, he surveyed the country, spying out suitable locations for the missions and especially a choice spot for a presidio. Then, using St. Denis as interpreter, he and the padres called the chiefs together and explained why the Spanish had returned and what they planned to do.

On July 3, 1716, Captain Domingo Ramón resolutely reclaimed Spain's rights to Texas. Within a week he established four missions, each strategically located near a river or stream and in the midst of a large Indian population. The first was San Francisco de los Tejas, its re-establishment being the fulfillment of Father Hidalgo's dreams. After twenty-three years of waiting he became its minister. Four days later and eight or nine leagues to the northeast Ramón founded La Purísima Concepción. By July 9 he was constructing Nuestra Señora de Guadalupe (at present-day Nacogdoches), and finally on July 10 San José de los Nazonis was underway.

San José was by no means the most important of these missions but its founding was typical. Located on Dill Creek (once called Bill's Creek), a tributary of the Angelina River, it was some twenty-one miles northeast of La Purísima Concepción, just within the northern boundary of what is now Nacogdoches County. Although it was in a densely wooded sector fed by numerous streams, there were nearby, Ramón noted, many fine ranches in the clearings and along the river banks. In fact, it was in the most heavily populated belt of the Nazoni and Nadaco tribes, the largest Nazoni village being in the immediate vicinity.

Soon after their arrival on July 10 Ramón and Father Isidro Félix de Espinosa, the well-known historian in charge of Querétarian friars, appointed Father Benito Sánchez to direct the mission. And before the day was over, the evangelical and civilizing transformation had begun—a governor, alcaldes, and other officials chosen for the mission village, the Indians constructing a church and log houses for the padres, soldiers directing work in the surrounding fields, the padres instructing the neophytes in the discipline of the church. What an exciting, fast-moving day it was for the Nazoni. Because of the Spanish they had received gifts, had participated in an election, had been reborn through baptism, and promised salvation.

But as in their prior attempt at colonization in Texas, the Spanish soon realized how difficult it was going to be simply to survive, how impossible to civilize and defend the area. Even establishing two more missions and a presidio nearby and, in 1718, a mission and presidio at San Antonio (a necessary halfway station for supplies and reinforcements) was not enough. With each passing day their existence became more unbearable, their position more untenable. In July Father Hidalgo was stricken with chills and fever; soon others, including Ramón, suffered equally serious ailments. By May, 1717, four had died, and there seemed to be no cure or remedy in sight. Hating the harsh climate and the lonely Texas frontier, some of Ramón's soldiers deserted, taking the best mounts with them. And once again, as in the 1690's, there was famine, both the bean and corn crops being dismal failures in 1717 and 1718. Faced with starvation if aid did not come soon, the mission fathers were reduced to eating crows in order to save their dwindling food supply.

And when a relief expedition led by Governor Martín de Alarcón finally arrived in October, 1718, with few supplies and only fifteen soldiers, the situation worsened. Morale, an increasingly serious problem over the past two years, almost ceased to exist. Gaunt and forlorn, the padres condemned the authorities in far-off Mexico City for their lack of support, for their apathetic attitude, for abandoning them in their time of need. The presidio soldiers, most of them ragged, undisciplined, and without mounts or arms, were a laughing stock, a pathetic excuse for protection. At San José, as Alarcón noted, the Nazoni had more weapons than the Spanish. If the French should attack or, for that matter, if the Indians should become hostile, who could stop them?

But most disheartening were the Asinais. It seemed that they, although not as fierce or nomadic as the Plains tribes, were just as uncontrollable and inexorable where Spanish techniques were concerned. The padres simply could not get them to congregate, to forsake their many gods and accept only one, to live the lives of Christians. During the past months the Spanish had found only two methods to control them—gifts or bribes and coercion by the soldiers. To the padres both solutions were unacceptable. But if they had been, the viceroy had made sure that neither one was available.

By late spring of 1719 many of the soldiers and settlers were urging the padres to abandon the East Texas missions, especially since the reasons for their establishment no longer seemed applicable. Then suddenly the French removed the question from the realm of academics. In June a small French force seized San Miguel de los Adaes, the mission that Ramón had established in 1716 some seven leagues from Natchitoches. Unknown to the surprised occupants, France had declared war on Spain in January, approximately six months before. For some inexplainable reason the Spanish government had failed to notify Mexico City; but now the word was out, and immediately there was panic. Pensacola had fallen in May; already a large French force from Mobile was marching against the other missions; the alternatives were to remain and face capture or to leave at once. So, despite the padres' protests and the pleas of the Tejas not to be abandoned to the French, Ramón ordered a retreat, and the Spanish withdrew to San Antonio.

It was not until the fall of 1720 that the Spanish decided to retaliate. But when they did, their move was impressive. The Marquis of Aguayo was the man responsible. Appointed Governor and Captain General of Coahuila and Texas in December, 1719, he was determined to drive the French from Texas, ready to sacrifice, he wrote the king, his "life, sword and property." Mainly at his own expense he assembled and equipped the largest expeditionary force for the northern borderlands since the days of Coronado and De Soto—4,000 horses, 1,500 cattle and sheep, 800 mules, and 500 men comprising eight mounted infantry companies.

After countless delays Aguayo finally left Monclova on November 16, 1720, eager and well prepared to chastise the French. By late December he arrived at San Juan Bautista where Father Benito Sánchez, the former padre of San José, joined him. Onward to San Antonio he proceeded, slowly but carefully fortifying it and the surrounding country against possible attack. On May 13, 1721, he moved eastward, his objectives being the East Texas missions and those who forced their abandonment. After an extremely exhausting march he reached the Trinity River where on July 25 the leader of the Asinai Confederacy and eight chiefs enthusiastically greeted him.

For the next two months Aguayo played many roles. To the Indians he was a combination god, friend, and benefactor. His praise was flattering, his repeated promise of protection comforting, his well-equipped army impressive. Yet what amazed them most were the gifts that he so lavishly heaped upon them. To the French, however, he was a relentless adversary, difficult to outwit, impossible to compromise. St. Denis, recently appointed the French commandant at Natchitoches, could get nowhere with him. Although informed by St. Denis that France and Spain had signed a truce, Aguayo ordered him to evacuate Texas immediately and permit the re-establishment of San Miguel de los Adaes; otherwise there would be conflict. Having an inferior force, St. Denis had no choice. But to the Franciscans Aguayo was a soldier-diplomat, a restorer of the faith, the foremost defender of the Spanish realm. For on August 2 the refounding of the abandoned missions began.

Father Sánchez was especially pleased. Proceeding to San José with a detachment of soldiers he rebuilt his church and lodgings. By August 12 he had congregated the Nazoni and was directing them in the routine affairs of mission life. Early the next morning amid great fanfare, Aguayo arrived with a company of soldiers and immediately displayed to the happy priest a real sense of the dramatic, indeed a necessary understanding of the Indian mind. While Sánchez was singing High Mass, Aguayo lined his men up in front of the church and at timely intervals had them fire salvos. Then, through an interpreter, he explained to approximately 300 Nazoni why he had come, and he authoritatively urged them to congregate, to live in the mission village, and to follow the teachings of the padres. In a grandiose manner he placed Sánchez in charge of San José, while to the Nazoni chief who was chosen governor of the proposed village he majestically presented—besides "a full dress of blue cloth"—a silver-headed cane, an official symbol of power and authority. Just before departing he distributed gifts profusely to all the king's loyal subjects.

When Aguayo left East Texas on November 17, 1721, the Spanish had complete control of the area. At the presidio of Los Tejas there were twenty-five soldiers capable of defending the missions and helping the padres in daily tasks. The Indians were friendly, many of them extremely fond of the priests. And as for the French threat, although St. Denis or "Big Legs," as the Asinais sometimes called him, was at Natchitoches, there was a Spanish garrison of 100 men opposite him at Los Adaes.

Yet during the 1720's the Franciscans experienced no better results than in their previous attempts. The climate was still hot and humid in the late spring and summer, damp and penetratingly cold in the winter; fever and crop failures were still the main commodities; Spanish officials in Mexico City were still indifferent or unsympathetic to requests for reinforcements and supplies; and the Indians still refused to congregate and accept instruction. No matter how hard the padres strove to win them over—ministering to the sick in their scattered villages, patiently learning to speak the many different native dialects, striving assiduously to show them a better way of life—they would not respond. After all, plowing or sowing in the fields was women's work, memorizing the *doctrina* was tedious and boring, staying within the village and mission day after day too confining. When Brigadier General Pedro de Rivera inspected San José, Concepción, and San Francisco de los Neches (formerly de los Tejas) in the spring of 1727, he found the mission villages abandoned, not even one neophyte on the premises. Nor would any return if the padres had to depend upon the presidio at Los Tejas; for the soldiers, Rivera disgustedly reported, were completely lacking in military discipline, often forgetting to post guards or to keep their weapons in good repair.

With such conditions prevalent in Texas presidios and missions Rivera recommended immediate retrenchment. Why expend money and manpower where neither the French nor Indians were threatening, where idleness was leading to corruption? On April 26, 1729, the viceroy agreed, and immediately the orders went out. Los Adaes, instead of having one hundred men, would be reduced to sixty; Los Tejas and its twenty-five-man garrison would be abolished altogether; and San José, Concepción, and San Francisco would have two soldiers assigned to each, subject to the padres' wishes.

Although the Querétarian friars had expected such a communiqué at some time after Rivera's visit, its appearance caught them by surprise. Distraught and alarmed, they hastily sent the viceroy a memorial, begging him to rescind his decree. How could they possibly remain in East Texas, they protested, unless there was military protection at Los Tejas? Without the garrison their effectiveness would be undermined, their safety endangered. How quickly the Indians would become insolent, defying the padres with petty thefts and then possibly with worse crimes. After all, they were better armed than the soldiers—the French had seen to that—and might at any time revert to their savage heritage. If this directive was going to remain the official policy, it would be much better, they asserted, to transfer the missions to more suitable locations where the padres could realize their full potential among more cooperative Indians. But if neither request were acceptable, they asked to be relieved of their obligations so they could return to their college at Querétaro for reassignment.

With Governor of Texas Melchor de Mediavilla y Azcona and Don Francisco Becerra, captain at Los Tejas, and the Guardian of the College of Querétaro also vehemently protesting, the viceroy decided to compromise. Since retrenchment was necessary, the padres must move to a new site. Already there had been recommendations to relocate the presidio of La Bahía on the Colorado River, so why not the three East Texas missions? During 1729 the viceroy sent small parties to find a spot where the climate was pleasant, the soil fertile, and the Indian peaceable. After receiving a favorable report from explorers and upon being assured by the padres that removal would not cost the king any revenue, he readily approved all suggestions, and by

July 27, 1730, San José, Concepción, and San Francisco
were established along the Colorado River (near Austin).

But for some reason, the missions did not prosper.
Apparently the Indians would not congregate. Or perhaps the area was not as hospitable as reported. In any
case, the padres in less than a year were asking to move
again, and Governor Mediavilla y Azcona was ready to
help. Personally examining several suggested sites, he
and Father President Fray Gabriel de Vergara selected
the new area for the three missions. To them it seemed
an excellent location along the San Antonio River, a
few miles south of the town. There the Indians were
more numerous, more willing to congregate, more
amenable to direction. In case of Indian attack there
was a well-fortified presidio within a few miles. Equally important was the fact that San Antonio was becoming a well-established outpost, known for its successful
missionary activity.

On March 5, 1731, Father Gabriel de Vergara and
Juan Antonio Pérez Almazán, captain of the Presidio of
San Antonio de Béxar, officially dedicated all three missions. At San Juan Capistrano—renamed to prevent
confusion with another San Antonio mission, San José
de Aguayo—the ceremony was in keeping with Spanish
tradition and psychology. With solemn magnificence
Almazán led the Indians into the surrounding fields
and, in the name of the king of Spain, loudly proclaimed
the land as theirs. So that they would feel that they
were taking active possession he had them perform
token gestures such as pulling weeds and moving rocks,
parodies on medieval feudal ceremonies. With equal
pomp he installed several Indian leaders as governor
and alcaldes for the mission village. Then the padres
took over, further delighting and impressing the Indians by performing a High Mass.

Quite different from its predecessor, San José de los
Nazonis, the new San Juan Capistrano had a much more
successful record. Although for five weeks enrolling

neophytes had been slow, sometimes discouraging work, Fathers Gabriel de Vergara, Pedro Muñoz, and Juan de los Angeles were exultant over the final results. The new recruits, members of the Pacaos, Pajalat, and Pitalaques tribes, unlike the Asinais, adapted readily to mission life. When the bells called them to chapel in the morning, they assembled without reluctance. When the padres repetitiously taught the *doctrina*, they were attentive and seemingly interested. In fact, in the routines of plowing and sowing, of helping the padres construct different buildings, of learning to care for the sheep and cattle, of digging wells and irrigation ditches, of performing countless chores, they seemed to be perfectly happy.

Within a short time the results of their efforts were quite apparent; the mission began to take shape. About one hundred yards to the west of the muddy San Antonio River, the chapel rose auspiciously out of the river's tangled, junglelike growth, dominating the cleared fields and grazing land to the north and east. Although rather crude structurally, it was typical of Spanish mission architecture. On the outside a heavy clay plaster hid the rough wooden base. Along the walls Roman archways were the basic design. A simple tower extended upward from the northern corner to interrupt an otherwise flat, almost oblong construction. To help the neophytes with their time schedule two bells in the tower's open arches regularly announced the daily routine. On the inside there were few improvements. A simple altar, crude frescoes on the walls, several canvas oil paintings, and three statues of Jesús Nazareno, Nuestra Señora del Rosario, and San Juan Capistrano were the main attractions of a drab, unimaginative building. But in the steaming, sultry surroundings of the San Antonio River bottom, the chapel must have been as impressive and awe-inspiring to the Indians as the burning bush was to Moses.

The other buildings were of similar structure and design—square or oblong, composed of wood and clay, plain and colorless. Just north of the chapel the neophytes' quarters, boxlike hovels with grass or thatched roofs, formed a part of the mission's west wall. The Indians' prior living conditions must have been poor indeed for them to accept such a meagre existence willingly. On the northern side a large granary was rather imposing, possibly built fortresslike at the mission entrance to discourage would-be attackers. South of the chapel was the monastery, commodious enough for the padres' needs, while next to it were the soldiers' quarters, sufficiently large to form most of the south wall and to house the three mission guards comfortably. Opposite the chapel to the east were open fields with only a high wall, approximately six feet in width, obstructing the view. At some future date the padres planned to strengthen the fortifications by building a large church, but for the moment it would have to wait.

Despite such promising beginnings at San Juan Capistrano and at the other San Antonio missions, the padres had to overcome many obstacles besides the climate and frontier conditions. The Indian menace was particularly trying. In the spring and fall of 1731 hostile Apaches raided the San Antonio area, wantonly stealing and killing. So bad did the situation become that by 1733 many of the mission Indians had deserted, especially after hearing that the Apaches had mutilated two presidio soldiers by stripping away and eating their flesh. At times the neophytes refused to venture forth from the mission compound, even "to watch the cattle," Father Vergara recounted, and then understandingly he added, "no one can blame them." For the next three years there were intermittent forays on the missions, although for a time an uneasy peace prevailed. But in the fall of 1736 an Apache chief, Cabellos Colorados or "Red Hair," attacked an escort train near San Antonio. A few days later he drove off forty horses from San Francisco de la Espada (formerly de los Tejas or Neches), a few miles south of Capistrano; and then he raided Capistrano itself, killing two Indian women in the attack. He continued to terrorize until December 11, 1737, when a Spanish expeditionary force surprised his camp and captured him.

In spite of such retaliatory measures the San Antonio missionaries lived in constant danger of attack, of hideous torture and death. Yet, from 1738 to 1746 they disagreed with the military and civil officials over the correct Indian policy. Men like Father Vergara and Father Benito de Santa Ana wanted to Christianize the Apaches, to build missions around their *rancherias*, to do what to many was the impossible—civilize them. Pointing to the Spanish-Apache campaigns of 1739, 1743, and 1745 as fitting examples, they argued that Apache thinking followed a simple pattern — force against force, counterattacks against Spanish attacks, inflicting ever bloodier reprisals upon their enemies. For instance, look what had happened after Toribio de Urrutia had scattered the Lipans and the Natagés in April, 1745, taking a number of them prisoner—immediate retaliation. Within three weeks nine people had been killed and every San Antonio mission except Concepción, where Father Santa Ana was in charge, was attacked. And if 100 mission Indians had not aided the garrison at San Antonio de Béxar on June 30, 1745, and if Father Santa Ana, by befriending the daughter of an Apache chief, had not neutralized part of the attacking force, some 350 Apaches might have pillaged and destroyed San Antonio and its mission system altogether.

A much more dangerous threat to the Franciscans, however, was Governor Carlos Benites Franquis de Lugo. Boorish, dictatorial, disliking anyone who questioned his authority, Franquis arrived at San Antonio on September 26, 1736, and during the entire year of his rule there was more than a misunderstanding between him and the fathers: there was unadulterated hatred. The Franciscans "were not the sons of St. Francis," he openly avowed, "but the sons of Satan." Let it be known that they wanted something and he would deny it; let them work on some project and he would do all in his power to discredit it. So that no one could misunderstand his feelings toward them, he withdrew two of the three guards from each mission. With "Red Hair" on a murderous rampage and with the soldiers essential for mission discipline as well as for protection, such an act, the fathers realized, was aimed at destroying their work.

Nor were the padres themselves beyond his wrath. For more than a year he accused them of every conceivable offense—of meddling in government affairs, of fiscal and moral dishonesty, of disloyalty to the crown, even of excessive cruelty to the neophytes. In August, 1737, a group of Indians from Capistrano and Concepción complained—at his instigation—that the Franciscans had abused them, feeding and clothing them poorly and resorting to the whip if they ran away or disobeyed. Although an ensuing investigation that proved the charges of misconduct were unfounded, the damage to mission morale was irreparable. Nor could it improve. For Franquis harried the padres continually, opening their mail and at times destroying it, transferring them frequently to different missions, and encouraging the neophytes to disregard church discipline.

When the viceroy finally removed Franquis in late October, 1737, the San Antonio missions were in bad repair. And during the next two years conditions became so desperate that the Franciscans had difficulty in keeping their flagging institutions from foundering. At Capistrano there were only twenty-three neophytes left by December, 1737. So the head padre, Father Mariano de los Dolores, asked the new governor for a ten-man military escort to help him retrieve the erring runaways. On March 24, 1738, after a three-week expedition he arrived triumphant at Capistrano, having persuaded 120 men, women, and children to return. Throughout 1738 and 1739 he continued searching for new initiates, trekking acros the Texas wilderness from village to village, offering the Indians a new way of life, and promising them salvation. For the time spent and the energies exerted, the results were often meager and discouraging. But Mariano persisted and endured. Even the frightful smallpox epidemic of 1739, when death and desertion reduced the neophytes at Capistrano from 218 to 66, did not dishearten him. Though exhausted and sometimes sick, he redoubled his efforts and Capistrano was maintained.

By 1741 Franciscan patience and perseverance were at last achieving desired results; Capistrano was becoming well-established. Living in the Indian pueblo were 169 neophytes who repeated the *doctrina* twice a day, who obediently followed the padres' directions in the fields and workshops, and who were either baptized or working toward that ordinance. Equally gratifying was the gradual transformation of the mission establishment itself. The chapel, while still rather crude, was acquiring the accouterments of tradition and time. Although there was no loom for weaving, the padres had added blacksmith and carpenter shops. Because of the five-mile-long viaduct constructed (for irrigation purposes) between Espada and Capistrano in 1731, they enjoyed bountiful crops of corn, beans, and melons. And as evidence of their increasing diligence there were more than 1,500 head of cattle, sheep, horses, and goats grazing in the nearby fields and woods, shepherded carefully by watchful neophytes.

For the next twenty years, despite frequent Apache raids, Capistrano continued to progress, and by 1762 the padres were extremely pleased with their accomplishments. Over the past thirty years they had baptized 847 persons and given Christian burial to 645. The number of neophytes had increased to 203, all of whom were baptized or were taking instruction. As for the mission's physical plant, besides gradually improving the already established buildings, the padres had built a small hall where the Indians wove cotton and woolen fabrics on three separate looms. While the Indian quarters were still much the same, still a squalid area of clay and plaster topped with thatched grass, there were plans for more adequate structures. The granary, filled with some 2,000 bushels of corn and beans, and the workshops, well-stocked with blacksmith tools and farm implements, were further indications of increased prosperity. But the real wealth was the livestock, the mission herds having grown considerably—1,000 cattle, 3,500 sheep and goats, 500 horses.

The early 1760's, however, represented the zenith, indeed the culmination of growth and achievement at Capistrano. After that, it and the other San Antonio missions declined rather rapidly. Maintaining adequate military and civil personnel on the northern borderlands was too expensive for Spain, Apache raids proving particularly costly and disenchanting. Yet, despite constant rumors of retrenchment, the Franciscan padres zealously worked among the Indians, continuing to fortify and sustain Spain's frontier outposts. Although paid only 450 pesos a year, they never lost their ardor even though the neophytes did. Constant discipline, laborious jobs, freedom-stifling and boring routines were more than they wished to endure. Whenever a soldier was abusive or mission punishment severe, whenever Apache incursions became alarming or dangerous, they ran away, relieved to escape the rigors of Spanish civilization. With each passing year the battle against human attrition—the padres' game of "capture the neophyte"—continued, the Franciscans' fight a losing one. In 1783 there were 99 neophytes at Capistrano; five years later only 33; and in 1790 a mere 21.

To close out Capistrano officially, for Spain to withdraw financial and physical support, only one step remained—secularization, a procedure well-known to the Franciscans. And on July 14, 1794, it happened. Arriving at Capistrano, Governor Manuel Muñoz instructed Father José Mariano Cárdenas to transfer immediately "all temporal property to the neophytes." With only twelve Indians listed on the mission rolls, the transfer was not a long, drawn-out procedure. Summoning the neophytes, Father Cárdenas read the secularization decree and explained what it meant. Then, within the next few days he had a surveyor mark off 12 plots of the best land nearest the mission, each 200 by 100 *varas*. After assigning each Indian a plot, he distributed the property stored in the various workshops—looms and spindles, farm implements, blacksmith tools, guns and ammunition. Next, he divided the cattle (the mission herd had dwindled to a mere fifty-five head) and arranged for equal shares on the soon-to-be-harvested crops. Before leaving he discussed with them what their new duties and obligations would be, trying to explain their future role in society, their life without Franciscan guidance.

For more than one hundred years after secularization Capistrano, neglected and unmourned, yielded to the climate and the environment. The descendants of the twelve neophytes continued to live in the area, anonymously existing from year to year, unmindful that a part of their heritage was crumbling away. Except for infrequent newspaper accounts stating that an inhabitant of Capistrano had married or died or committed some felony the mission went almost unmentioned. The chapel was rebuilt in 1907, along the same specifications as the original, but otherwise there was little improvement or upkeep.

Being off the main highway, hidden in the San Antonio River bottom, Capistrano has not changed much from early frontier days. As it was in the nineteenth century, neglected and in need of repair, so it is today. The rustic chapel still exists, with services being held every Sunday morning; the monastery, although well-roofed, is a barren and empty shell; the other buildings have broken, crumbling walls, pock-marked by weather and time; and the mission compound is seemingly on the verge of succumbing to the weeds and dense thickets near the river. Yet for the visitor who seeks Capistrano, who turns off the main highway some seven miles south of San Antonio onto a narrow, dirt road, who suddenly views the ruins of the mission compound and the tower chapel emerging out of a maze of trees, there may be a moment of pause, of reverence, even as it was for the first neophytes. For here is a reminder of Spain's greatness, a monument to the patient, heroic efforts of those padres who helped conquer and civilize this land, of man's indomitable spirit. Indeed, Capistrano is part of our heritage.